Professor Errare Presents....

Stuff You Should Know

Professor Errare
and
S. Will Campbell

Published by Shawn Campbell

Professor Errare Presents....Stuff You Should Know

1st Edition

ISBN: 978-1-7332314-3-5

To Herodotus, for proving to the world that fact finding is not necessarily a necessity for writing history.

A Note to the Reader

This book should be considered a form of parody and satire created for reasons of entertainment only. In other words, only an idiot would use this book for any type of serious citation. While Professor Errare strives to only provide factual information on the historical things you should know contained in this book, his research methods are somewhat questionable given that each part only got about an hour's worth of internet searching. As well, at times certain facts have been written about in a manner, which while entertaining, may have twisted and stretched the truth just a bit. If you find anything in this book interesting, Professor Errare strongly encourages you to do your own research. The internet represents the greatest source of knowledge in human history, maybe try using it for more than just cat videos and porn, and of course, cat porn videos.

It's important to remember while reading this book that history is a god awful mess that just straight up doesn't give a shit about your personal beliefs or ideologies. While written history is often put together in a way meant to jerk off one group or another, ignoring any facts that might ruin said jerking pleasure, true history is a total fuckfest of contradictions and illogical spit takes.

For anybody who has been on social media these days, it should be pretty obvious that a lot of shit is happening. Unfortunately, people seem to be going at this shit with little to no knowledge of any historical context whatsoever. To help with this human shortcoming, Professor Errare is proud to present this volume detailing stuff (apparently you can't use shit in the title and be considered a respectable publication) you should probably know regarding how we got where we are today. It covers a little bit of everything, but hopefully after reading it you're poor decisions will at least be well-informed poor decisions.

#1 Synthetic Shit

By the time the mid-19th century rolled around, many of the great thinkers of the day began fearing that the end was near. Thanks to the advent of modern science, the world's population had topped one billion people for the first time. However, the understanding of how the world worked had also grown to the point that those who did the math began to predict that it wouldn't be long until farms could no longer keep up with the growing demand for food. Basically, the amount of certain needed nutrients in the soil was limited, chief amongst them being nitrogen.

Now throughout most of history, nitrogen got into the soil via the creatively named nitrogen cycle, whereas various bacteria fixed nitrogen from the atmosphere and rotting dead plants and animals in the ground, which then became available for plants to use. From the age of the earliest civilizations, this natural process was aided by farmers via the application of livestock shit directly onto fields. However, shit also contained a lot of salt, meaning it could damage the soil if too much was put on at a time, and by the 19th century the demand for food was growing beyond the yields which shit could provide.

In the early 1800's it was discovered that certain types of bird and bat shit, called guano by the classy, had amounts of concentrated nitrogen far above that of the livestock shit, with much less salt, meaning guano could be used to greatly boost crop yields. As a result, by mid-century these deposits, which were mostly on scattered islands near the equator, were quickly being claimed by any nation that had the power to do so. The super shit that was guano allowed food production to keep up with population growth through the end of the century, making many individuals, and several countries, fabulously wealthy. Of course, as goes with anything like this, there were all sorts of human rights abuses and even two separate wars in South America over guano deposits.

When the mining of guano began, many of the islands had piles of shit on them more than 150 feet deep, with birds and bats continually working to replenish them even as they were mined. However, by the start of the 20th century, the scientists of the world again came to the conclusion that the end was near. Guano deposits were beginning to run low, and new sources of mineralized nitrogen found in Chile's Atacama Desert would not be enough to both make up the difference and the growing demand. It was at this time that a German scientist by the name of Fritz Haber entered the scene.

For the scientific world, the global food problem had a simple answer. They just needed to get their hands on more nitrogen somehow to boost yields. This problem was especially maddening given that 74% of the frickin atmosphere was nitrogen, but it was inaccessible due to it being a gas and a bunch of other issues involving chemistry. It was Fritz Haber who came up with the answer in 1909. Haber, being one smart schmuck, figured out a method to harvest nitrogen from the atmosphere by putting it at a high pressure and temperature in a steel tank and then injecting hydrogen. The resulting chemical reaction created liquid ammonia, known as nitrogen trihydride by sciency folks, which made for a perfect fertilizer.

Haber's method, which became known as the Haber Process, was seen as nothing less than a god damn miracle. No longer were humans constrained by the natural nitrogen cycle. For the first time they could make as much nitrogen fertilizer as they could ever need. Over the proceeding decades, billions of tons of nitrogen fertilizer were produced, allowing significant increases in crop yields, which in turn allowed the human population to reach 7 billion and beyond without the ever present threat of mass starvation. While the increased use of nitrogen fertilizers has undoubtedly caused issues for the natural world, it is undeniable that our society today only exists because of them. So, there you go, magically sucking fertilizer out of the air. One of the greatest inventions of all time.

#2 The Man Who Didn't Need Any Bullshit

Fritz Haber was a Jewish man who was born in the mid-nineteenth century. If you have no idea what any of this is about, you should probably go back and read the preceding article. Anyways, Fritz's father, Seigfried, was a merchant who sold dyes and paints, and also pharmaceuticals for some god unknown reason, because who the hell wouldn't buy medicine from the guy also selling you the paint to slap on your house? Fritz's mother was a woman named Paula, who was also Siegfried's first cousin. This was heavily frowned upon by the Haber family. At that time in Germany, fucking your first cousin was considered an absolute necessary for the aristocracy, and a common regrettable reality for the poor, but it was just not something those in the middle class were supposed to be doing. Either way, Fritz had a fairy normal childhood for the time, including the premature death of his mother. As far as being Jewish in Germany went, it was about one of the best of times to be alive, with the country generally just accepting that Jews were people like everybody else. Crazy, I know. Wanting his son to be as educated as possible, Siegfried sent Fritz to top colleges in Berlin to study chemistry, though perhaps it was just part of a scheme to get the boy to develop new paints/medicines for him to sell. Whatever the reason, Fritz excelled in school, eventually graduating with his doctorate. While he did work with his father for a time, the two did not get along, and eventually Fritz took a job with a university.

Now at the time, as those who read the preceding article would now, the scientific community was trumpeting warnings that the world was soon to end. Growing populations were soon expected to outpace the world's ability to produce food, and nothing but dire consequences were expected. One of the biggest things holding farmers back from growing more food was the availability of nitrogen in their soils, a problem farmers mostly met by spreading bird and bat shit, called guano, on their fields. However, by the start of the twentieth century, the demand for guano was far outstripping the ability of birds and bats to shit it out.

Now of course the world had no shortage of nitrogen. After all, 74% of the frickin atmosphere was made up of it. The problem was how the hell does one get nitrogen gas into the soil? Nitrogen was a tricky element, its molecules tended to like to stick together, making converting from a gas to anything else tricky as shit. Frtiz, being an especially stubborn fellow, spent seventeen years working on the problem, eventually developing the Haber Process in 1913, which used high pressure and temperature to convert nitrogen and hydrogen into ammonia, a liquid that could be put on fields. The invention of the Haber process effectively made nitrogen fertilizer an unlimited resource, depending upon the price of energy, which in turn allowed the human race to avoid mass starvation and create the world we know today.

Unfortunately, this is where Fritz's story kind of goes off the rails. The next year World War I broke out with all of Europe descending into chaos. Aside from being a great scientist, Fritz also considered himself a German patriot. Putting aside his efforts to better the world, he switched over to helping Germany win the war. His first great contribution was to show how the Ammonia created by his Haber Process, while good for making fertilizer, also could be used to make explosives, thus allowing Germany to build munitions even though its ports were blockaded. His second great contribution was the development of poison gas for the war. Despite the disapproval of military generals, Fritz convinced Germany's leaders to use poison gas in the trenches. He personally attended the first use of poison gas in a battle, and reportedly got such a patriotic boner over the whole thing that he soon after held a party at his home to celebrate. His wife, also a well known chemist, less than pleased with the nightmare her husband had unleashed, shot herself that very night. Unbothered, Fritz left a few days later to oversee further poison gas attacks.

After the war, in 1919, Fritz received the Nobel Prize in chemistry for the invention of the Haber Process, a controversial choice given the fact that he had created one of the most horrifying weapons in history. Unfazed, Fritz was put in charge of a scientific institute and began trying to figure out a way to make gold out of sea water in order to pay off the reparations Germany was forced to make after the war. While there are trace amounts of gold in ocean water, they are quite small and almost impossible to separate from other elements. His work failed, and ultimately, being a Jew, he was forced to resign as head of his institute and flee from Germany when the Nazis took control of the country in 1933. Not being the favorite of anybody, what with the whole poison gas thing, Fritz spent the next year traveling from one country to the next across Europe. This couch surfing ruined his health and he died in 1934.

However, even dead, Fritz still had one last terrible thing to add to his legacy. One of the last projects that Fritz oversaw as the head of his institute was the creation of a pesticide for killing insects in granaries called Zyklon A. The Nazi's later took this pesticide, removed the harsh smell meant to warn people that it was a poisonous gas, renamed it Zyklon B, and used it in the gas chambers in their death camps. So yeah......shit.

#3 Watergate Part 1

In 1971, the New York Times and the Washington Post released a set of documents known as the Pentagon Papers, which showed that the both the Kennedy and Johnson administrations had lied extensively to both Congress and the U.S. public concerning the Vietnam War. For the then sitting president, Richard Nixon, the smearing of the reputations of the past two Democratic presidents was a god send. However, it was also a little problematic given that for any president the widespread publishing of classified documents was not really a good precedent to have set. As a result, Nixon attempted to block the further release of the papers via a court order, though ultimately he failed when the Supreme Court ruled against him. Having tried the legal method, Nixon then switched to illegal tactics, putting together a crack team of ex-investigators which he tasked with the job of discrediting the source of the Pentagon Papers leak. This group called themselves the White House Plumbers, because they were tasked with plugging leaks. The Plumbers were so proud of their name that they put up a sign in their office, though they soon after took it down when someone pointed out that maybe advertising their existence was pretty dumb. So you know, maybe crack team wasn't exactly the best description for them.

Anyhow, the Plumbers basically failed at their assigned task and by the spring of 1972 all of them had been reassigned to Nixon's re-election campaign, which compared to doing illegal espionage was pretty fucking boring. However, being go-getters, they decided that the best way they could help their boss get re-elected for a second term was to break into the Democratic National Committee offices at the Watergate Building and put some illegal wiretaps on the phones. Not wanting to get their own hands dirty, the Plumbers hired a rag tag group of five Cuban Freedom Fighters to do the break in on May 28, paying them with campaign funds. Amazingly enough the breaking in portion of the plan went off without a hitch. Unfortunately, the planting of the bugs didn't go so well. As a result, a second break in took place on June 17, which ended with the five men getting arrested after a security guard found duct tape on all the door latches.

Given the whole illegal wiretapping thing, the FBI soon after began investigating the crime. It didn't take them long to connect things to the Plumbers given that one of the Cuban freedom fighters had their names in his address book. Given that the Plumbers were all working for the Nixon re-election campaign and were using campaign funds for illegal activities, this caused a bit of a panic that worked its way to the senior levels of the Nixon administration and clear to the president himself. This panic wasn't helped by the fact that within days of the break in the Washington Post started reporting that the arrested men had connections not only to the Plumbers and the Nixon re-election campaign, but also some higher level Nixon administration officials. This information came from a source that the paper called Deep Throat, after a popular porno movie of the time, who in actuality was a high level member of the FBI.

Nixon, not known for being the most level headed of men in the best of times, shit his pants with panic. Not only could a connection between the burglars and his administration and campaign risk his chances of re-election, but it also threatened to bring to light all the other less than legal activities the Plumbers had done over the years. With straight up murder not really being an option, Nixon instead went with trying to derail the investigation by having the head of the CIA imply to the acting head of the FBI that the whole thing was a clandestine CIA operation and a matter of national security. The head of the FBI thought this was bullshit, but wanting to keep his job, personally destroyed some evidence connecting the five burglars to the Plumbers and began giving daily updates of the investigation to the White House. Nixon then had his aides promise to pay the legal fees of the five burglars and the Plumbers in return for keeping their damn mouths shut and lying under oath if necessary. Where did this money come from? Campaign funds of course.

The summer of 1972 was a strange one. As the FBI investigation continued, making greater and more complex links between the burglars and the Nixon re-election campaign, all dutifully reported to the Washington Post via Deep Throat, Nixon and his aides worked over time to distance themselves from the criminal activity. However, the bad news kept rolling in. In September, the FBI reported that the Watergate break in was part of a massive campaign of political spying and sabotage on behalf of the Nixon campaign. The five burglars, several Plumbers, and several key members of the Nixon campaign were all indicted. However, none of it mattered at all due to the fact that Nixon's opponent in the 1972 election was a man named George McGovern, a far to the left wingnut, at least for the time, whose running mate had been hospitalized for depression on numerous occasions. When faced with deciding between a man who surrounded himself with crooks and a crazy man who surrounded himself with more crazy people, the American public went with the man surrounded by crooks. In November, Nixon won re-election by the widest popular vote margin in American presidential history, winning all but one state.

#4 Watergate Part 2

By the start of 1973, old Tricky Dick Nixon was feeling pretty damn good. Not only had he managed to win re-election by one of the biggest landslides in American history, but he had also managed to contain the damage caused by the Watergate break in to a couple of bungling burglars and few idiotic members of his re-election campaign, all of whom had either plead guilty or been convicted by January without a single one implicating anyone within the Nixon administration. With the scandal firmly behind him, he could get back to concentrating on leading the country forward. Oh wait, that's not right, things actually blew up in his fucking face.

Nixon's problems began again in February when he attempted to reward the acting head of the FBI by having him made into the permanent head of the FBI, a process that required a series of confirmation hearings before the Senate. Not really being all that good at such things, the acting head let it slip that he had been providing the White House Counsel, a man named John Dean, with daily updates throughout the Watergate investigation and that Dean had probably lied to the FBI. Unsurprisingly, the acting head of the FBI did not get confirmed. This was soon after followed in March by one of the convicted White House Plumbers writing a letter to the case's judge claiming that he had committed perjury on the orders of high level Nixon administration officials. As a result, the Justice Department began looking deeper into the whole mess, quickly finding more Plumbers that were willing to implicate White House officials, key amongst them Counsel John Dean and the Chief of Staff.

It was at this point that Nixon in effect began a cover up of the cover up. At the time nobody was sure how high things went and there was no evidence to connect the president to the dirty dealings of the past year. To save his own ass, Nixon began setting up several of his aides as scapegoats. This didn't sit well with sacrificial lamb numero uno, John Dean, who began secretly working with Justice Department investigators. However, this was far from being a smoking gun since Dean refused to tell all he knew, hoping to use his information as leverage to avoid prosecution. By the end of April, the Justice Department informed Nixon that they had enough evidence to implicate seven of his aides, including John Dean, in a cover up. Nixon responded by firing the seven aides. However, his trouble was far from over. At the same time, the acting head of the FBI let it slip to a Senator he was friends with that he had been ordered by Dean to destroy evidence. The Senator, not being a piece of shit, leaked this to the press.

Throughout all these shenanigans, the source in the FBI known as Deepthroat continued to leak information on the investigation to the Washington Post. As a result, the Democrat majority Senate created a special investigation committee in mid-May, and two days later the Justice Department appointed a Special Prosecutor who would work outside the normal Justice Department hierarchy to investigate possible crimes by Nixon. The Democrats turned the Senate committee's investigation into political theater, televising every meeting for all the world to see. By June, John Dean was willing to admit that he had discussed the cover up with Nixon on numerous occasions, but other than his testimony, which Nixon's allies claimed was just Dean trying to get himself out of trouble, there was no evidence. The hearings dragged on with no progress.

Things finally changed in July when a former low level Nixon aide revealed that all conversations and phone calls in the Oval Office had been tape recorded since 1971. Both the Senate and the Special Prosecutor subpoenaed the tapes, but Nixon refused to hand them over, citing executive privilege. With no other options, the subpoenas started grinding their way through the court system and gradually the public began to lose interest. Even as all this was going on, a separate investigation was taking place concerning Vice President Spiro Agnew for taking bribes nearly a decade ago while an official in Maryland. Under mounting pressure, Agnew resigned in October, leaving the Vice Presidency vacant. Seeing an opportunity, Nixon went to his Attorney General and demanded that he fire the Special Prosecutor. In what became known as the Saturday Night Massacre, the Attorney General refused, instead choosing to resign, as did his second in command. The third in command did as he was told. The move outraged Nixon's opponents and the majority of the public. To try and smooth things over Nixon went to Disney World and gave his famous "I'm not a crook" speech. When that didn't work, he was forced to tuck his tail between his legs and allow the appointment of a new Special Prosecutor just eleven days after firing the first.

#5 Watergate Part 3

In the last month of 1973, Congress confirmed the appointment of Gerald Ford as Vice President. He was considered a compromise candidate, seen as not being in Nixon's camp but also being too weak willed to seek the presidency for himself. By the start of 1974, the pressures of the continued Watergate investigation were beginning to take their toll on Nixon. He was losing sleep and drinking heavily, and many of his aides were privately discussing what to do if Nixon had a mental breakdown. To make matters worse, the new Special Prosecutor was even more willing to play hardball against Nixon than his predecessor, opening lines of investigation into Nixon's accepting of gifts while president and possible tax evasion.

In March, seven former Nixon aides were indicted by a grand jury based on evidence collected by the Special Prosecutor. The indictment included a sealed document that named Nixon as an unindicted co-conspirator. In the end, the Special Prosecutor had persuaded the grand jury not to indict Nixon, claiming that a President could only be indicted after leaving office. Instead, the sealed document was delivered to the House Judiciary Committee which sat on it for more than a month as they reviewed its contents. Though the House was majority Democrat at the time, many of the committee's members felt that there was not enough evidence to overwhelm Nixon's support.

Things changed in April. The Special Prosecutor was finally able to get the courts to order Nixon to hand over the White House tapes. However, instead he released 1,200 pages of transcripts edited for curse words, of which there were plenty. As the battle raged on, the American media and public poured over the released transcripts. Though they contained no smoking gun, they did create a picture of a devious and immoral man who was contemptuous of his own country, its institutions, and its people. Nixon's public support collapsed, the House Judiciary Committee began impeachment hearings, and prominent members of Nixon's own party began suggesting that he should resign. The battle over the tapes and Nixon's executive privilege stretched all the way to the Supreme Court, which by the end of July, in a unanimous decision, ordered Nixon to release all of the tapes. It proved to be the end for the beleaguered president. Amongst the tapes were recordings that showed that not only had Nixon known about the break-in since just a few days after it had happened, but that he had also personally okayed legal payments to the five burglars in exchange for their silence.

Soon after the release of the tapes, the House Judiciary Committee voted to impeach the president on the grounds of obstruction of justice, abuse of power, and contempt of Congress. If it was passed by the full House, then the Senate would be able to impeach the president by a two-thirds vote. Republican leaders met with the president and told him he most certainly would be impeached if he didn't resign. Drunk and tired, Nixon took their advice and resigned on August 9, the first president to ever do so.

With Nixon's resignation, the impeachment hearings came to an end, but possible criminal investigations continued. However, these were ended when Gerald Ford granted Nixon a presidential pardon in September. Though Ford claimed he did it so the country could move on, critics argued that Ford had promised the pardon to get Nixon to resign. The whole mess resulted in a new investigation by the House Judiciary Committee, but in the end nothing came of it. In total, 69 members of the Nixon administration and re-election campaign were indicted, of which 48 spent time in prison. The whole episode soured the public on the Republican party, allowing the Democrats to increase their majorities in both the House and Senate. The Democrats would maintain their majority in the Senate until 1981 and in the House until 1995 (though to be fair they had held majorities in both since 1955). The Democrats used their greater majorities to pass several bills limiting executive power, all of which would later be walked all over or ignored by both Republican and Democratic presidents. Due to the unpopularity of his pardon of Nixon, Gerald Ford lost the 1976 presidential election to Jimmy Carter. Prior to Nixon, both Kennedy and Johnson had recorded many of their conversations. After Watergate, not a single president has supposedly taken back up the practice. Nixon spent the rest of his life claiming his innocence, dying in 1994.

#6 Anita Somebody To Listen

In 1991, President George Bush the Elder got the opportunity to nominate a second Supreme Court justice during his term of office, a move that pundits claimed would surely swing the court into a conservative madhouse that would likely completely demolish all that the liberal left held near and dear. It goes without saying that Bush faced a bit of an uphill battle, what with the Senate being controlled by the Democrats at the time, so he decided to throw his opponents a curve ball of conflicting ideals. The person Bush nominated was named Clarence Thomas, a conservative black man who though once having been the head of the Equal Employment Opportunity Commission (EEOC), the government body tasked with fighting discrimination in the work place, had a long record of criticizing affirmative action. He was also seen as an opponent of abortion for some reason, though at the time he had never been quoted on the topic. Overall Clarence was also a bit of a strange choice given that he had only served as a judge for sixteen months, but Bush figured that they could use Clarence's reputation as being an all around good guy to get past that little problem. Despite declarations by opponents that it would be a bloody brawl, Clarence's confirmation hearings were pretty tame, with most questions centered around whether or not he thought of himself as a libertarian. With no smoking gun beyond the fact that he was a conservative, Clarence's opponents really had no way to stop him, and as the hearings wound down it was considered certain that he would get Senate approval.

That all changed when Anita Hill entered the picture. Anita was a former employee of Clarence's who had worked with him a decade prior in the Department of Education and the

EEOC. Anita, along with most people who had worked with Clarence, had been interviewed by the FBI as part of the nominee's background check. Though Anita had told the FBI that Clarence had sexually harassed the shit out of her, the information was not disclosed to the public, at least until near the end of the hearings when some mysterious person for totally no political reason whatsoever leaked it to the press. Clarence's opponents lost their collective shit and the hearings devolved into a crazy ass circus with some demanding Clarence's nomination be blocked because he was a sleazebag and others declaring Anita to be a lying bitch. Eventually, the FBI was forced to reopen its background investigation into Anita's claims, and she was invited to testify.

Anita's accusations did not paint Clarence as an all around swell guy. Anita stated that the harassment had happened over a two year period, starting with Clarence asking her out on dates, and when she refused, devolving into weird sexual comments. These ranged from talking about pornographic films showing group sex and bestiality, to very detailed descriptions of how awesome Clarence was in bed and what shape he preferred a woman's ass to be. However, by far the strangest claim involved Clarence asking Anita if she had a put a pubic hair on his can of Coke. Clarence was given a chance to refute such claims, which he did, adding in the idea that Anita's testimony was all just a crazy conspiracy cooked up by Democrats who only wanted a black person to succeed in politics if he fully agreed with their agenda. Both sides marched out further witnesses to testify to the good character of both Clarence and Anita and both sides attacked those they saw as countering their view of what had happened.

Despite resulting in several Senators having to utter the porn star name Long Dong Silver on the record, in the end the whole thing boiled down to a he said she said situation. Though there was a second woman claiming to have been harassed, she was never called to testify. The Democrats believed that the second woman was a less reliable witness since she had been fired by Clarence for misconduct. Doubts were also raised about Anita given that she had chosen to follow Clarence from the Department of Education to the EEOC, which Anita stated was due to her believing in her work and the false hope that the harassment would end. In the end, the Senate approved Clarence by a vote of 52-48, the closest Supreme Court appointment in a century.

In the following years, more women came forward to accuse Clarence of sexual harassment or to corroborate the accounts of other women, but it was too late. However, the public outcry over the whole mess was too great to ignore. The accusations had turned sexual harassment into a nationwide discussion. Within months of Clarence being appointed to the Supreme Court, President Bush signed a bill giving victims of sexual harassment the right to sue the shit out of their harassers. Harassment complaints filed with the EEOC shot up 50 percent and companies around the country started requiring sexual harassment training. The next federal election in 1992 resulted in a significant upsurge in the number of women in Congress, a trend that has continued to grow to this day.

#7 Worms of the South

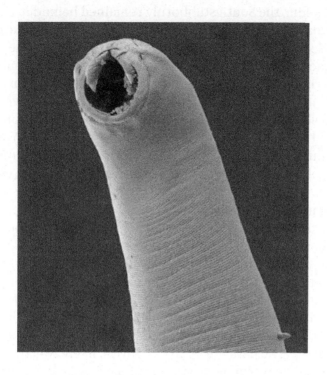

Quick, if somebody asked you to describe stereotypes for people from the South, what would you say? Did you say dumbass lazy uneducated hicks? Well congratulations, you're a fucking terrible person. Wait you might answer, look at all of this data I looked up on my phone showing the southern states have some of the highest poverty rates and lowest test scores in the nation. Good for you, but did you ever stop and wonder why things are that way? No? See, like I said, terrible person. Well, strap in buddy, it's time for a little edumacating.

Though you can certainly find a few nutjobs, most people can agree that the end result of the Civil War was a good thing. The United States remained a single country and slavery was no longer a thing. However, just because overall something is good, doesn't mean that some of the finer details can't be shitty. For instance, it should really be no surprise that the Civil War really fucked up the South. The combination of the Union armies burning everything they could get their hands on, large amounts of property being seized without compensation, and a good chunk of the population of working age men being killed, led to a complete economic collapse. To which the U.S. responded by pretty much saying, "fuck you, you got what you deserved, good luck with all that." A significant portion of the southern population, white and black, was left poor as hell, by which I mean being able to read was seen as a rich man's trait and things like wearing shoes and not shitting in the woods were considered luxuries. So you know, not good.

Well, fast forward to the start of the twentieth century, and large parts of the South were still just as bad as they had been at the end of the Civil War. Even as the United States went through an economic boom, the South stubbornly remained behind in all areas of development. Given that it had been forty years since the war, the educated masses of the time just kind of decided that the South was still poor as shit partly due to their backward way of thinking, but more importantly because they were just plain genetically inferior, this being a time when the idea of eugenics was all the rage. After all, anyone traveling through the South was sure to see thousands of slack jawed yokels, hunched over on porches, scratching their pot bellies, and staring at nothing. Sure, there were some up and coming people down there, but most were idiots. Well, one doctor from New York, a man named Charles Stiles, didn't think genetics was the reason. In 1902, he did some actual scientific research, and lo and behold he discovered the culprit. A little parasite called a hookworm.

The hookworm is an interesting character who infects people by hanging out in the grass waiting for somebody to step on it. Once stepped on, the hookworm burrows its way into your foot, starts drinking your blood, and then releases its eggs back into the wild via your shit. Funny thing about hookworms, since they drink copious amounts of blood, people suffering from them often develop symptoms like insatiable exhaustion, trouble thinking, hunched shoulders, and distended bellies. Symptoms can be even worse in children, with stunted growth and delayed cognitive development commonly occurring. You can probably see where this is going. Dr. Stiles discovered that 40 percent of the Southern population was infected with hookworms. The parasite, native to Africa, likely was brought over by the slave trade, where it thrived in the warm moist climate of the South. It was especially prevalent in poor rural areas where a combination of people going barefoot, poorly built outhouses, and free roaming livestock created perfect conditions for hookworms to spread, all things that became extremely common after the Civil War.

So, problem solved. Not really. The Southerners, already living with the stigma of being lazy idiots, didn't really appreciate the added stigma of being riddled with parasites. Real attempts at eradicating hookworms didn't begin until 1909, thanks to funding from the billionaire John D. Rockefeller. Doctors roamed the countryside, letting people peer through microscopes at their own shit, handing out free medicine, and giving tips on ways to avoid infection, such as wearing shoes and building better outhouses. Unfortunately, Rockefeller's efforts only lasted five years, because rich people get bored easily, and though other programs continued the fight, hookworms would remain an issue in the South for decades, not really being brought under control until indoor plumbing and wearing shoes became common place by the 1950's. Given that this was the United States in the twentieth century, it should go without saying that campaigns to eradicate hookworm mostly focused on the white population, which wasn't all that great for the black population. A population which not only had to deal with a bunch of shitty segregationist laws and policies keeping it poor as shit, but also increasingly the stereotype that they were all lazy idiots, you know, just like the Southern whites had until someone started getting rid of their hookworms. Yeah, that's where that fun little stereotype came from too. By 1985, hookworms were all but gone from the South. Today, it's one of the fastest growing economic areas in the country.

#8 The Corn Disease

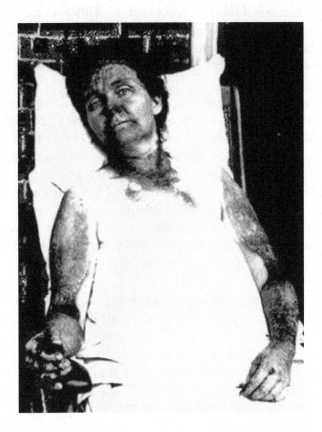

Some 9,000 years ago, farmers in southern Mexico first domesticated a type of grass which eventually became the grain we now all call corn. Thanks to it being easy to grow and having high yields, corn quickly spread across the Americas, becoming the staple food supply for countless Native Americans. When Europeans first arrived in the Americas, they at first avoided corn, believing that they were technologically superior because they ate a wheat based diet, which makes absolutely no sense whatsoever. However, over time they eventually gave up on such high ideals, bringing it back to Spain where it quickly spread to Italy, West Africa, and then across Europe and eventually the world.

Though corn was eventually widely grown around the world, it was not seen as a staple crop for many centuries. This began to change as the increasing world population made it more difficult for people to grow enough food. In the late nineteenth century, many areas in Europe switched completely from wheat to corn, taking advantage of the yellow grain's higher yields, with northern Italy especially taking advantage. While things at first seemed to work out just fine, in the 1880's an epidemic of some new and terrible disease broke out, infecting hundreds of thousands of people. The disease started with people developing a terrible rash and diarrhea, and ended with dementia and death. So you know, not really that great of a situation. The scientists of the time, not being complete idiots, noticed that the disease, which they called pellagra, based on some Italian words, only affected those who had switched over to a corn diet. As a result, they decided that the corn must have some toxin in it that made people sick if too much was eaten. This was somewhat confusing given that the Native Americans had been eating large amounts of corn for centuries, but the scientists just basically declared "eugenics" and went with it. This led to a decline in corn consumption and a campaign to end the planting of corn in France.

While all of this was going on in Europe, people in the United States continued to eat corn as happy as you please, with little to no ill effects. However, this all changed in 1902, when pellagra appeared in the South. By 1906, it was full blown epidemic, affecting hundreds of thousands of people and killing tens of thousands each year. The sudden outbreak stumped scientists because it made no damn sense. The people in the South had long used corn as a staple in their diet; the Southern diet of the time mostly involving cornmeal, meat, and molasses; and the pattern of infection seemed to affect certain groups at random. The most common groups to get pellagra were the poor, orphans, prisoners, and people in mental institutions, with women being especially susceptible. To further confuse things, the disease was not found in other nearby groups, such as prison guards.

Though the pellagra epidemic was killing thousands of people every year, the U.S. government didn't get around to doing something about it until 1915. Backed by government funding, a man named Dr. Joseph Goldberger, began to study pellagra, and not being a complete idiot, quickly connected the problem to a diet too dependent on corn. Dr. Goldberger showed that eating less corn could cure pellagra, a declaration the Southern politicians reacted to by telling him to fuck right off. The people of the South were already dealing with widespread poverty and stereotypes about them being lazy idiots, so the added on idea that they had terrible diets was just a little too much for the Southern leaders to swallow. As well, the majority of poor people in the South lived on small plots of land, and the only way they could feed themselves was by growing corn. Even if the politicians had been supportive of change, it wasn't like anybody had the money to improve diets, given that the South was poor as shit and the U.S. government had no interest in helping them out.

Undaunted, Dr. Goldberger continued his research to try and identify exactly what needed nutrient was missing from the Southern diet. Unfortunately, he died in 1929 without figuring it out. However, in 1937, other scientists connected pellagra with a niacin deficiency. As it turned out, Native Americans had long soaked their corn in lime because if they didn't the body was unable to digest most of the niacin in corn, something they had forgotten to mention while they were dying of Old World diseases and being murdered for their land. As well, the outbreak in the U.S. could be tied to the introduction of a new corn milling process in 1900 called degermination. By removing a part of the corn kernel called the germ, corn would last much longer in storage, but at the loss of all the nutrients in the germ, including niacin. This loss was just enough to tip the balance and cause the pellagra outbreak. Finally, women were more susceptible because the estrogen in their bodies limited niacin intake. In 1938, the U.S. began a program of fortifying various foods with niacin, which resulted in the end of pellagra as a public health risk.

#9 The Great Fat Cover Up

By the time the mid-1950's rolled around, the American scientific community was becoming increasingly alarmed at the growing trend of people dying of heart attacks. Society was changing quickly. Where once people had mostly lived in rural areas doing physical labor each day, the modern American was urban and desk bound. Though advances in medicine were rapidly doing away with the threat of infectious disease, long the number one killer, heart disease was rising rapidly. Luckily, one Minnesota scientist, a man named Dr. Ancel Keys, believed he had the answer. Dr. Keys was one of the first to note that the rise in heart disease in the U.S. correlated quite well with a rise in meat consumption. The American economy was booming, and as American's became wealthier, they were stuffing more meat down their gullets. In 1955, with absolutely no proof whatsoever, Dr. Keys went before the World Health Organization and declared his lipid theory, which stated that dietary fat raised cholesterol, which in turn increased heart disease. According to Dr. Keys, the only way to reverse the terrible trend was for people to switch a large part of their consumption of animal fats to healthier vegetable oils.

In 1958, in an attempt to actually prove his theory, Dr. Keys launched what became known as the Seven Country Study, one of the largest dietary studies in history. While Dr. Keys collected massive amounts of data, he also hit the road, promoting his lipid theory throughout the 1960's. Though the general public was less than interested, the scientific community largely embraced the lipid theory, especially as several smaller observational studies were released supporting it.

It was at this point that a man named Dr. Ivan Frantz entered the picture. Dr. Frantz, also from Minnesota, was a colleague and fervent supporter of Dr. Keys' lipid theory. In 1968, wanting to forever end debate on the subject, Dr. Frantz concocted one of the most precise dietary studies in history. The problem then, and still today, with dietary studies was that they were based off of observational studies, where volunteers kept food journals that reported what they ate. These studies had a significant problem in that it was not unusual for people to forget and/or lie when recording what they had eaten. Dr. Frantz got around this issue by not using volunteers, but rather 9,500 mental patients housed in Minnesota's psychiatric wards. Since the diet of the patients was controlled, Dr. Frantz could easily randomly assign half a diet high in animal fats and the other half a diet high in vegetable oils. Since this was the 1960's, the state officials running the psychiatric wards were perfectly a-okay with all of this.

In 1970, Dr. Keys released the results of his Seven Country Study, which lo and behold proved his lipid theory utterly and completely correct. The idea that high cholesterol caused heart disease fully entered the public sphere; and health organizations, the U.S. government, and oilseed farmers began a concerted effort to get people to switch from animal fats to vegetable oils. As a result of these efforts, consumption of red meat and animal fats began to decline and consumption of vegetable oils increased. It was perhaps the largest and most rapid shift in American diets in history.

Dr. Frantz was eager for his study to be the proverbial nail in the coffin of animal fats. However, when he started going through his data in 1973, he found things not to be as expected. While the vegetable oil group most definitely did have lower cholesterol levels, their risk of dying of heart disease actually increased. This left Dr. Frantz in a befuddled mess, at least until a group of Australian scientists released a long-term observational study supporting the lipid theory later that year. With such further evidence available, Dr. Frantz assumed that he must have fucked up his own study somehow, put all of his data in his basement, and forgot about it.

The lipid theory remained concrete science for the next forty years, a period that saw vegetable oils become a significant portion of the American diet. However, cracks began to appear in the claim in 2011, when a scientist found Dr. Frantz's data and published the results, causing a huge stir in the scientific world. This was followed by a review of both the Australian study and the all important Seven Country Study, both of which revealed that data had been left out that would've supported Dr. Frantz's findings. Forty years of dietary advice had been built on a house of cards. While scientists continue to disagree on what this all means, it is worth noting that the decline in animal fat consumption resulted in an increase in sugar consumption, since vegetable oils tend to taste like garbage on their own. This increase has been tied to rising obesity and diabetes rates. Happy eating.

#10 Welles's War of the Words

It's supposedly a well known story. In 1938, Orson Welles and his Mercury Theater radio show decided to jazz things up a bit by doing a modern day rendition of the famous book "War of the Worlds" by H.G. Wells. The book, only forty years old at that point, told the story of a Martian attack on London. Aside from being a pretty heavy analogy on British imperialism, it was also dull as hell. Though lots of different people claim credit for coming up with the idea, it was eventually decided to present the story via a series of fake news casts interrupting a pretend show playing music. By which I mean the cast and crew, shitting their pants over how completely boring the story was going to be, just kind of threw together a cockamamie scheme right before the broadcast began. For the listeners at home, a brief announcement that the upcoming story was completely fiction was followed by 40 uninterrupted minutes of pure lunacy. Through the fake news bulletins, the radio show followed the fictionalized account of a strange cylinder landing near the real town of Grover's Mill, New Jersey. Eventually the cylinder opens, revealing Martians, who start killing people willy-nilly. The army is sent in, but is defeated, people rush to flee the onslaught, and the Martians attack New York City. All pretty standard science fiction for the day.

Now according to the stories spread about the broadcast, Americans at the time were apparently stupid as shit. Taking the radio broadcast to be real, millions of people across the country panicked. People reportedly fled their homes en masse, running from the coming Martians. Bands of armed men roved the streets. Some people became so hysterical that they had heart attacks, while others contemplated suicide in order to end things on their terms. Phones at police stations and newspaper offices rang constantly, and hospital waiting rooms were overwhelmed by people injured in the wild flailing around of society. The newspapers the next day were filled with hundreds of such stories from across the nation. American's demanded Orson Welles' head for the stunt, and he was forced to issue an official apology. Today it stands as one of the greatest stories of mass hysteria in American history, which it is, just not in the way you think.

If you haven't guessed the premise of all this yet, then you might have fallen for such shenanigans if you lived back then. That's right. It was almost all completely bullshit. To start, not many people actually tuned into the radio show. The Mercury Theater wasn't that widely listened to because it was in the same time slot as one of the most popular shows on the radio at the time, which starred the ventriloquist Edgar Bergen. That's right, the most popular radio show of 1938 was a ventriloquist act. I'll let that sink in for a moment. Okay, back to business. So again, not very many people even listened to the broadcast of War of the Worlds, and even fewer actually panicked. Now that's not to say that some didn't. After all, the United States had a population of 130 million people back then, just based on statistics there were bound to be some idiots. There were some reports of panics. For instance, across the nation the occasional person did call in to their local police, newspaper, or radio station to ask if the radio show was real, especially from listeners in New Jersey. As well, in Grover's Mill, New Jersey, purported center of the invasion, a couple of drunks did go out with rifles and shoot at the town's water tower. So yeah, there were definitely some idiots out there, but a bunch of idiots out there is pretty different than an entire country freaking the fuck out.

This was something that Orson Welles figured out pretty quickly after his initial apology. In interviews afterwards he pretty much said the whole thing was overblown and ridiculous, though later in life he himself did play it up as some grand wide reaching scheme that he cooked up for publicity. According to the newspapers of the day, the panic was proof of how easily the new fangled thing called radio could manipulate the public. In truth, it was actually proof of how easily journalists could do the same, conflating a couple of random reports into a nationwide story. To understand why the newspapers would do such a thing, one only has to understand what was happening within the industry. Newspapers, once the only source for news in the country, were facing increasing competition from radios and movie theater news reels. Readership was declining, which meant advertising revenue was doing the same, and some pundits were predicting the eventual end of newspapers all together. It was pretty much the same as when newspapers print disparaging articles about the internet.

Outside of the newspaper accounts, there exists little to no proof of any kind of panic. A researcher did put together a study in 1940 suggesting millions freaked out, but later critics pointed out that the study was pretty much just made up. As for the newspapers, they kept hammering on the story for about three weeks, with a number of stories bluntly claiming that radio listeners were all mentally deficient, but finally abandoned it to go back to actually reporting on things like the real news. However, by that time the story had reached Adolf Hitler in Germany, who mentioned the so-called panic in one of his speeches as an example of the decadent corruption created by democracy. As for Orson Welles, the whole mess catapulted his career, allowing him to secure funding for a little film called "Citizen Kane", which became one of the most famous movies in history.

#11 My Dad Is Genetically Superior To Your Dad
Part 1

In the mid-nineteenth century, a German monk by the name of Gregor Mendel began experimenting with pea plants, which eventually led to him becoming the father of modern genetics. Now of course at the time the idea of creating better animals and plants via breeding was not a new idea. For thousands of years people had known that if you get two superior plants or animals to have sexy time then you have a chance of creating a new even more superior plant or animal. However, Mendel was the first to understand the whole idea that such things were caused by genes that could be passed on both actively and recessively. Of course, this amazing discovery was completely ignored for thirty years, and Mendel was largely forgotten until the start of the twentieth century when his findings were re-discovered.

It was an interesting time for science. A growing understanding of the natural world had resulted in significant advances in industrialization and medicine, resulting in a rapid exponential growth in the human population never before seen in history. However, this same growth in science also resulted in a better understanding of the affect people had on the environment, resulting in many predicting that it was just a matter of time before there were so many people that everything just kind of collapsed, resulting in the end of human civilization. Given that this was the thought process of many of the leading minds when genetics became a thing, it's not hard to see how some crazier ideas began to take shape, key amongst them the theory of eugenics, which is just a sciencey way of saying breeding people like animals.

Now the idea of eugenics is nothing new. Throughout human history, groups have been rather less than kind to those deemed to have physical or mental handicaps or deficiencies. However, the modern idea of eugenics stemmed from a man named Francis Galton, who was a cousin of Charles Darwin. A big fan of his cousin's theory of evolution, Galton took it a step further by claiming that pretty much all human traits were hereditary, and therefore if you wanted better people, all you had to do was control which ones were allowed to fuck. It's probably worth mentioning that when it comes to physical traits, Galton wasn't wrong. However, Galton also claimed the same was true for things like intelligence or just being a nice person.

Now at the time, Galton was one of the most respected scientists in the world, being one of the first to apply large-scale statistics to world issues. His accomplishments included creating the first weather map, devising a method to classify fingerprints, calculating the optimal method for making tea, inventing a whistle for hearing tests, and statistically proving that prayer did diddly squat to help people. Through years of rigorous statistical study, Galton became convinced that people who did better in society did so because they had superior parentage. While such theories were fully embraced by the rich and powerful, for reasons that should be obvious as shit, it really didn't take off until the early twentieth century when people first began to fully understand the idea of genetics.

For the first time in history, those who were economically better off finally had what they thought was scientific proof of what they had always thought was true. Namely, that they were genetically superior to everybody else, and would be regardless of education or living conditions. These members of the upper crust, rather excited over such things, threw massive amounts of money to spur on further research on how great they were, effectively creating a new academic discipline at universities around the world. In thanks, the researchers at these universities threw themselves fully into studying the effects of genetics on social standing and the rise and fall of societies and civilizations. Things of course got pretty fucked up.

#12 My Dad Is Genetically Superior To Your Dad
Part 2

In the early twentieth century, eugenics was a rapidly growing and accepted science in the world of the intellectuals. Thanks to money and support from the rich and powerful, most major universities had programs for eugenics research and many organizations worked to sway public opinion in favor of its teachings. Thanks to the idea of eugenics, the wealthy and successful no longer had to feel bad for those beneath them, for their right to their stations in life was preordained by evolution and provable by science. After all, if two wealthy and successful people had a child, wouldn't that child also turn out to be wealthy and successful? Such was the popular thinking of the time. Of course, not all people were quite so convinced by such so-called research, but you can probably guess which side got the lion's share of the research funding.

As part of the so-called great leap forward, many pro-eugenic scientists and organizations began pushing for policies that would put their beliefs into practice. The first target were the mentally handicapped and insane. As studies began to show that mental illness could be passed down to later generations, laws began to be passed allowing for the forced sterilization of those in state mental institutions. One of the first countries to adopt such policies was the United States, with California at the forefront of new eugenic laws, but such policies quickly spread across most of the developed world. Eugenics was seen as a progressive cause, with its main opponent being the Catholic church, which ironically argued against the movement on the basis that the body was sacred and that control of one's body should lie with the individual. In some countries, including some U.S. states, sterilization policies were eventually expanded to include people with low IQs, criminals, and in some cases those born with genetic physical disabilities.

As time went on, the eugenics movement quickly expanded to judging entire groups of people as inferior rather than just certain individuals. According to research just as flawed as everything else the eugenicists produced, entire races of people were genetically inferior, as could be shown by their level of economic development. It should come as no surprise which racial groups got the shitty end of that stick. Such racist beliefs had been around long before eugenics, but with the so-called trials of scientific rigor suddenly applied, it became much more okay to push through some truly shitty laws and policies.

What followed was a truly insane amount of circular thinking. For most countries in Europe and North America, the widespread belief in eugenics raised concerns over racial purity. These claims were used to pass numerous racist, segregationist, and anti-immigrant laws. The purpose of these laws was to keep the blood lines of the so-called Nordic race, people whose ancestors came from western and northern Europe, as pure as possible. It was all exactly as fucked up as it sounds. Similar policies were followed in Japan, though of course those policies focused on the idea of the genetic superiority of Japanese people over everybody else. In Brazil, things took a decidedly different turn, with the dominant white minority enacting eugenic policies meant to encourage intermarriage in order to breed out the declared bad traits of the black population. Similar policies were enacted in Australia regarding its aborigine population.

As the idea of eugenics became more mainstream throughout the developed world, its claims became much more widely believed. Raising the quality of a country's genetic stock was seen as paramount for not only its continued existence, but for the overall success of humankind. The embracing of eugenics was seen as the final shaking off of the old rituals of the past in order to embrace the shining golden age of a scientific future. It was seen as human civilization breaking itself free of the shackles of the natural world, taking control of its own evolution. Those deemed unfit would be left behind, the harm to them not mattering since they were of inferior stock anyways. Few other ideas have ever sprouted so much evil.

#13 My Dad Is Genetically Superior To Your Dad
Part 3

To understand the fucked up things that happened next, one must also understand that throughout the earliest twentieth century there was a widely held belief that humankind was on the brink of a Malthusian collapse. Rapid increases in the consumption of natural resources, caused by rapid population growth and industrialization, was expected to outstrip the ability of the planet to produce said resources by the second half of the century. While many believed that such issues could be overcome by embracing scientific progress, many others contended that the self-destruction of society was inevitable. All the progress that had been made in the preceding centuries would be lost as the world was swallowed by famine, plagues, and warfare. Such thinking helped spur on a new age of imperialism at the end of the nineteenth century, with countries vying to claim as much territory as possible to ensure they controlled enough resources to survive the coming cataclysm. The belief by many that such conflict was inevitable was what turned the belief system of eugenics from another terrible point in history to one of the most horrifying chapters of all time.

The economic collapse which became known as the Great Depression rattled every bit of society. Eugenics was not immune. With so many once wealthy and successful people cast down into what they once would've considered poverty, people began to more greatly question the idea of economic value being a proxy for human worth. However, many of the larger ideas of eugenics had become so embedded that they were hard to shake off. The Great Depression was also seen by many Malthusians to be the start of the long expected societal collapse. As a result, some people began to meld the theory of evolution and the ideas of eugenics with the overall idea of a nation-state. Whereas in many nations the rise of nationalism was centered on the idea of moral superiority, these thinkers added in the idea of genetic superiority as well. As in nature, only the strong survived, which meant that it was okay to do anything in order guarantee the continued existence of the nation. While supporters of such ideas remained the minority in most countries, in others, such as Germany and Japan, they became the dominant force with terrible consequences.

For both Germany and Japan, the starting of World War II was an effort to secure enough land and resources to guarantee the survival and expansion of each country's declared master race. In the case of the Japanese, the view of other groups as being inferior resulted in the murder of around 6 million people in China and southeastern Asia via civilian massacres. Germany, as we all know, was much worse. Germany was the culmination of the ultimate idea of eugenics. From the moment the Nazis took control of Germany, they began a policy of ethnic cleansing that increased in brutality and efficiency as time went on, eventually resulting in the establishment of death camps to do away with the undesirables. This list included Jews, Roma, the disabled, gay men, Poles, and Slavs. Some 17 million people were estimated to have been killed directly by the Nazis, with millions more killed by policies that restricted food and medicine to those deemed less than human. It was to be just the beginning. Plans for after the war called for depopulating huge areas for future German expansion. Though eventually won by the Allies, World War II resulted in the death of some 85 million people, four percent of the world population.

The horrors of the war, combined with the terrors revealed during the Nuremberg Trials, ended the widespread belief in the need for eugenics. The once lauded ideas that had shaped the world, began to crumble and fall away over the next several decades, replaced by an increased sense of the sanctity of an individual's right to exist. This helped push forward many movements, including the end of Imperialism and many Civil Rights movements. Beginning in the Great Depression, and really hitting its stride in the 1950's, new research better highlighted the importance of environment on human development. Genetic research eventually showed no major differences between the genetic codes of people of different nationalities and races. Though many of the policies once supported by the eugenics movement have been swept away, the after effects of the era continue to haunt global society to this day.

#14 The Washington Redskins

By the 1930's, professional football was all the rage. Wanting to get in on the action, a businessman in Boston named George Marshall founded a new team called the Boston Braves, which he creatively named after a baseball team with the same name which shared the same stadium. The baseball Boston Braves were named in honor of Tammany Hall, a political organization that dominated New York City politics, which in turn was named after a Native American chief named Tamanend, who had been pretty chill towards the white guys who founded Philadelphia. Confused yet? Good. Anyways, Marshall needed a logo for his team. Being a lazy bastard, he just copied the picture on the nickels of the time, which had a random Native American head on one side and a buffalo on the other. You can probably guess which side of the coin Marshall picked. Unfortunately for Marshall, nobody seemed to give a shit about his new football team. Convinced that sharing a name with a baseball team was just too confusing, because people often get baseball and football confused, he decided to change the name. The name he chose was the Redskins, mostly because he could save a bunch of money if he didn't have to change the logo. The change in names did little to help the team, which was soon after moved to the nation's capital where they became the Washington Redskins.

Now during this time things were not all that rosy for actual Native Americans. The tribes were all living on reservations and it was common practice to take native children from their parents to be educated at boarding schools where they would learn to be more white. So yeah, just a bit fucked up. However, mixing together children from a myriad of tribes did have the positive affect of giving a sense of Native Americans being a group rather than just a bunch of tribes. This eventually led to the creation of the National Congress of American Indians (NCAI) in the 1940's. The NCAI mostly concentrated on some pretty big issues unrelated to this story, but they also fought against the use of negative Native American caricatures. Such as calling your team the Redskins and promoting it via a myriad of terrible stereotypes. Unfortunately, nobody gave a shit, at least until the 1960's when the Civil Rights movement made an increasingly large number of white people aware that maybe treating entire groups of people like shit wasn't all that awesome.

The use of negative caricatures became a bit of a big deal, so much so that the Redskins decided that it might just be best to sidestep the issue. In 1965, they changed their logo to a spear, and then later a big letter R with some feathers on it. However, they didn't change their name. This lasted until about 1971, when deciding they missed their old logo, the Redskins went to the NCAI and asked for permission to start using it again. Amazingly enough, rather than telling the Redskins to fuck off, the NCAI instead decided to give their approval, apparently being happy with the whole thing as long as it was done in a respectful manner. It was a controversial move, especially within the Native American community, but overall it mollified the angry white people who mostly moved on to be outraged over whatever the new thing to be outraged over was.

It's probably worth stopping real quick here to ask where the hell the term redskin came from given that Native Americans most definitely are not red. Well, originally a tribe in what is now known as the southeastern U.S. called itself the red people, a name derived from the tribe's creation myth. The Europeans of the time, who were all about simplistic color coordinated differentiation, just kind of took this and made it a common term for all Native Americans, which made no sense whatsoever. Whether or not the term is racist has been debated ever since, but it has been widely used by racist people, which is really not a point in its favor. However, such debates were largely ignored in relation to the Washington Redskins until the 1990's when a group of Native Americans sued to have the team's trademark removed under a law that said people couldn't trademark racist terms. The natives originally won in 1999, but the decision was overturned in 2005 under a technicality that basically centered around the fact that all of the plaintiffs had been adults in 1971, meaning that if they had a problem they should've brought it up then. To get around this, a younger group of Native Americans sued in 2014, and again the trademark was removed.

It was at this time that The Slants entered the picture. The Slants were an Asian-American band who wanted to trademark their name. However, the government denied them the right to do so stating that the term was totally racist and that The Slants were bad people for wanting to have such a trademark. This didn't sit well with The Slants, who appealed the decision all the way to the Supreme Court, which found in a unanimous decision in 2017 that trademarks are free speech protected under the First Amendment. The basis of the argument was that it was not the government's place to decide what speech was offensive and what was not. As a result of this decision, the Washington Redskins got their trademark back, though of course it is still controversial as fuck.

#15 Three-Fifths

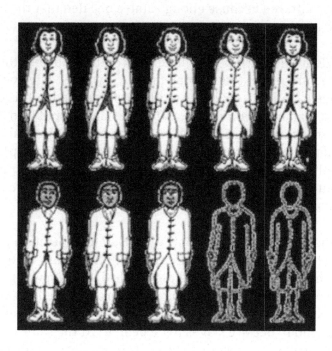

By 1780, the Revolutionary War was wrapping up with it being pretty obvious that most likely the British were not going to hold on to what they called the thirteen colonies. With victory pretty much guaranteed, the thirteen colonies, who now thought of themselves as the thirteen states, decided it was about damn time to set up a federal government in order to guarantee the British had no chance of ever coming back. What they ended up creating was a states' rights advocate's wet dream known as the Articles of Confederation, wherein each state regardless of size had one vote in Congress which had the power to do absolutely diddly-squat. It worked exactly as well as one might imagine, leaving the federal government broke pretty much immediately. Since the government having no money is kind of a problem, some of the more centralized thinkers of the day proposed an amendment wherein each state would be taxed according to the value of its real estate. However, this being the 18th century, a time when such calculations were a huge pain in the ass, the proponents of creating a federal tax soon shifted to the idea that the taxes should be based instead on the number of people in each state, a much easier calculation, or at least it seemed.

Certain things were easy to agree upon. For instance, all thirteen states agreed that Native Americans were totally not people so should not be counted. However, where they ran into a problem was how to count slaves. Now at the time, only three states had ended slavery; Massachusetts, New Hampshire, and Pennsylvania; but overall the southern states had a literal shit ton of slaves compared to the north, around a ratio of 7 to 1. As a result, the northern states were totally down with the idea of including slaves in the count of population for tax purposes, while the southern states pretty much said no fucking way. This led to

Congress making one of the strangest compromises in history, wherein they decreed that each slave would only be counted as three-fifths of a person. So yeah, pretty fucked up. However, none of this mattered because enough states decided that the idea of a federal tax was stupid and so the amendment never passed.

The Articles of Confederation continued to be the law of the land over the next decade, during which time the number of states outlawing slavery rose to five with the addition of Connecticut and Rhode Island. It's probably worth mentioning that this didn't mean that slaves were freed, just that any children born after the ban was put into effect wouldn't be slaves. The idea was that slaves were property and you couldn't just take people's property away, even when said property were god damn human beings. Again, pretty fucked up. Anyways, eventually the whole mess that was the Articles of Confederation was so close to collapsing that the states agreed that a new government was needed, resulting in it being replaced by the U.S. Constitution in 1789.

Now of course with the Constitution the whole idea of state population is rather important, what with it dictating how many votes each state gets in the House of Representatives and to elect the president. This of course re-ignited the whole debate on whether or not slaves should be counted. However, this time the opinions were reversed. In a rather ironic twist, the southern states, who pretty much thought of slaves as being the same as cattle, wanted the highest law in the land to declare slaves to be people. At the same time, the northern states, who were waking up to the fact that slaves were totally people, wanted the highest law in the land to view them as property. So yeah, seriously, super fucked up. Anyways, the debate over how to count slaves almost completely sank any chance of forming a new government, at least until the old three-fifths compromise was remembered, which was still just as exactly terrible as it was when it was first come up with a decade earlier.

As a result of the three-fifths compromise, the southern states got around a third more presidential electors and seats in the House of Representatives than they otherwise would've had. This allowed them to exert a much greater amount of control in the federal government, including putting in place pro-slavery Supreme Court Justices and ensuring that the number of slave states always remained close to the number of free states, which helped the shitty policy of slavery continue long after the majority of people in the country decided it was fucked up (70% of the non-slave population lived in the free states by 1860). This unbalance eventually culminated in the shit show known as the U.S. Civil War. Now one might wonder why the northern states agreed to such a shitty deal. Well first, they were quite literally afraid of the country ripping itself apart while still in its infancy, something that continually came close to happening over the next 70 years until it actually did happen with the aforementioned war between the states. Second, while the southern states did get more political power, they also had to agree to the same population counting method if the federal government ever imposed a national tax. This was favorable to the northern states, many of whom were hoping to see such a national tax enacted. Spoiler alert, it never was, mostly thanks to the increased political power of the southern states. So yeah, not the best moment in American history.

#16 Sex Cults and Silverware

In the 1840's, John Noyes was a young abolitionist preacher in Vermont with a bit of a problem. His poor wife, a sickly woman, had suffered four miscarriages and doctors warned that another failed pregnancy would likely kill her. Understandably not wanting to kill his wife, but still liking the whole idea of sex in general, Noyes began to explore alternatives, the majority of which involved just fucking other women. Now being a preacher and all, this left John with a bit of a theological conundrum. After all, pretty much all religious figures of the day agreed that sexing it up with random women was rather frowned upon by god. John dealt with this dilemma by declaring that god was totally okay with it as long as you didn't ejaculate. Why this might seem like a rather strange solution to some, John was apparently one of those people who thought life was more about the journey. Not surprisingly, a lot of men in the area were totally down with this new idea of what was okay with god. Amazingly enough, a lot of women were okay with it too, probably because it gave them an opportunity to actually enjoy sex without the complicating factor of having a baby.

In 1844, John formed his first Christian commune in Piedmont, Vermont. The Piedmont commune was like many utopian communes of the day, in that the community collectively owned property, women were thought of generally as equals to men, and slavery was heavily frowned upon. What made the Piedmont commune different was that everybody lived in a big house together and was free to have sex with whomever they chose, as long as nobody ejaculated. To make sure that the ejaculation rule was obeyed, members who failed to hold back were reported by their partners to John, who then led a public shaming wherein the guilty party would be stood before the community and criticized for their lack of control.

Things went on this way for about four years until John was caught fucking the wife of a man who was not a part of the commune and who was most definitely not down with some random guy doing his wife, even if said random guy wasn't ejaculating. John was arrested on charges of adultery. Released on bail, he and his followers soon after fled Vermont to New York, where they founded a new commune known as the Oneida Community.

In New York, John decided to double down on his whole belief system. Declaring that possessiveness and exclusive relationships were the way of the devil, marriage was abolished and members of the commune were encouraged to have sex with everybody and anybody. While men were still expected to avoid ejaculation, women were expected to enjoy sex as much as possible, though in John's view this included only having limited rights to refuse a man asking for sex. Women were also given equal status in the commune. They were allowed to cut their hair short and wear pants. As well, the raising of children was seen as a community responsibility, giving women within the commune the opportunity to try their hand at every available job.

It should come as no surprise that the Oneida commune was quite successful. Membership rose to several hundred people and money came in via the manufacturing and sale of various goods; such as leather bags, silverware, palm hats, animal traps, and garden furniture. With everything going so well, things of course had to get weird. John became obsessed with the sex lives of his followers. Under his orders, those who had sex had to report it to a special committee which kept meticulous records to make sure nobody was developing any undue attachments to a single person. Over time this committee grew in power until rather than just reporting sexual exploits, people instead had to first ask its permission before engaging in the dirty deed, and eventually it just told people who to have sex with. Older women, who had less of a chance of getting pregnant, were ordered to have sex with younger men, starting at the age of 14, in order to help educate them on how to avoid ejaculation. The younger women were saved for the older men, who were seen to have the most ejaculatory control. Pretty much all of the virgins were deflowered at the age of 14 by John himself. Eventually, this all culminated in John ordering certain people to have children together in order to create what he hoped would be perfect people. The perfect children were kept separate from their parents and taught to avoid all attachments except to the community.

Things began to fall apart in 1879. Forewarned that the state of New York planned to arrest him for oh so just so much statutory rape, Noyes fled to Canada, never to return. He died there in 1886. With the loss of John's leadership, and most of the original members of the commune growing old, the younger people in the group broke away to live more traditional lifestyles. The commune broke up in 1881, with its property and manufacturing businesses converted to a joint stock company called Oneida Limited. This company eventually came under the leadership of Pierrepont Noyes, one of the perfect children, who focused the company solely on the manufacture of silverware. Oneida became the largest producer of silverware, dinnerware, glassware, and kitchen tools in the world for most of the twentieth century. Not bad for a company that started as a weird sex cult.

#17 The Trail of Tears

By the start of the 1820's, the old native tribes of New England and the Midwest had largely been scattered and driven westward across the Mississippi. Having allied themselves with the British in the American Revolution and the War of 1812, they found few supporters to help them resist the growing encroachment of European settlers upon their lands. Seeing the fate of their northern brethren, the five main tribes in the southeast; the Cherokee, Choctaw, Creek, Chickasaw, and Seminole; instead mostly chose a route of assimilation. Through a series of treaties, they established independent territories within the United States. In return, members of the tribes converted to Christianity, formed centralized governments, and shifted their way of life to more closely match that of their new European neighbors, including the owning of slaves. Unfortunately, these attempts did little to slow the progress of European settlers, who were eager to claim new lands for settlement. As a result, both the Creek and the Seminole fought against the Americans, a decision that led to both tribes being forced to sign treaties surrendering wide swaths of territory. Unfortunately, the opening of these newly captured lands for European settlement only increased the tensions between the tribes and their new neighbors, creating a rift between

That same year, Andrew Jackson. and the newly made southeastern states. Tensions were only and Seminole wars, both of which he largely spent lands in 1828.

Jackson had long been a proponent of moving the southeastern tribes westward, necessarily out of a sense of hostility towards the tribes. In Jackson's view, the tensions between the states and the tribes would continue to grow, eventually leading to a conflict that the tribes would undoubtedly lose due to their smaller numbers. If the federal government tried to intervene on the behalf of the tribes, there was a risk that federal troops would have to fight the state militias, which may cause a civil war. In Jackson's opinion, it was better to remove the tribes to federal lands west of the Mississippi where they would be left alone and no longer in conflict with hostile state governments. In order to do this, Jackson pushed the controversial Indian Removal Act through Congress in 1830, which gave him the ability to negotiate with tribes for their removal westward.

The Choctaw nation, centered in central Mississippi, was the first group to agree to the removal. Though reluctant to do so, the Choctaw were convinced it was in their best interest to make the trade. Starting in 1831, some 17,000 Choctaw made the journey, leaving in November so they could plant crops in the spring. Though initially well supplied by the government, a much more severe than expected winter and an outbreak of cholera killed some 4,500 people. It was a disastrous start, which caused the other tribes to resist attempts to get them to voluntarily move. Similar to the Choctaw, the Chickasaw, who lived in northern Mississippi, reluctantly signed a treaty agreeing to removal in 1832. However, the decision was more contentious, and it took years for the removal to begin. The Chickasaw finally moved west in 1837. Of the 3,000 who made the journey, some 500 died. The Creek, who lived in central Alabama, were also forced to sign a treaty agreeing to the removal in 1832. However, they largely chose to remain, putting them in increasing conflict with encroaching settlers and the state militia. This eventually led to the outbreak of some violence in 1836, which the U.S. government used as an excuse to forcefully remove the Creek that same year. Under military escort, some 15,000 Creek moved westward. An estimated 3,500 died along the way.

Negotiations with the Seminole did not go as well as the other tribes. Though a few agreed to the idea of relocation, most refused to budge, preferring to take refuge in the Floridan Everglades. This resulted in a war which was fought from 1835 to 1842. Bolstered by freed slaves, some 3,000 Seminoles fought against a U.S. military expedition that eventually reached 40,000 in number. Though around a thousand or more were eventually relocated westward, the remainder fought on until the American government eventually gave up on the war, leaving the few hundred members of the tribe left to live as they wished in the swamps.

The last tribe to be removed were the Cherokee. The Cherokee were split on the idea of removal, though most were not in favor. Negotiations between the Cherokee and the U.S. stretched on for years. In 1835, the U.S. signed a treaty with them which ... refused to ... when he became Cherokee, claiming that they represent up with any further delays, Van Buren sent in the U.S. some 2,000 spring of 1838 and forcefully moved the Cherokee to internment camps where disease ran rampant. The Cherokee were kept in these camps until the fall of 1838, when agreeing to stop resisting, they were allowed to make their way westward. Severe winter weather caused further death on the journey. In total, some 4,000 Cherokee died in the removal.

In the proceeding decades many more tribes were removed to what became known as the Indian Territory from across the Midwest, Great Plains, and Southwest. Eventually large amounts of this land was seized by the U.S. government in 1887, which then in turn opened up large amounts of it to white settlement. Today we call it Oklahoma.

#18 Tulsa's Shame

The discovery of oil at the turn of the twentieth century in Oklahoma turned the little hamlet of Tulsa into a thriving boom town overnight. Tens of thousands of people flocked to the city, overwhelming the Native Americans who made up the majority of the population. Would be entrepreneurs from the urban centers of the Midwest and East Coast, many of them immigrants, mixed with poverty stricken Whites and Blacks from the South, making Tulsa one of the most diverse cities in the region. For the arriving Black population, Tulsa represented an opportunity for economic success, but also a chance to escape from the violence of the Jim Crow south. Though the ugliness of segregation followed them to Tulsa, the newly arrived Black population still found economic success in the neighborhood of Greenwood. By 1920, Greenwood was the most affluent Black neighborhood in the country.

In 1921, a young black shoe shiner went across the street to use a segregated washroom on the top floor of a downtown office building. On his return, he tripped while exiting the elevator and fell into the young woman working as the operator. Some of the local shop owners heard the woman scream and called the police, claiming that an attempted rape had taken place. The police, not being total idiots, took this claim with a grain of salt. However, since the woman was saying little about the incident and the shop keepers were pretty insistent about their version of events, the police decided that it would probably be best to take the shoe shiner into protective custody. It's probably worth mentioning that at the time racial tensions were at a rather high level. Barred from serving in the military, African-Americans had been one of the primary sources of alternative labor during World War I, taking over many of the jobs that had been held by the 4 million or so young men who were drafted into the military, many of whom were the children of poor immigrants. On the one hand, this created new opportunities for the nation's Black population, who prior to the war had almost entirely worked as sharecroppers in the South. On the other, it caused issues for the returning soldiers, who came home to find a new source of competition for the jobs they had left behind. Matters were only worsened by a post-war recession and many big companies bringing in Black labor to break up worker strikes. As a result, a series of race riots broke out across the country in the summer of 1919, with immigrants attacking Black neighborhoods. Though Tulsa largely remained peaceful, there was an undercurrent of violence both actual and threatened. Thousands of Whites in Tulsa joined the newly formed Ku Klux Klan after the war, and six Black men were lynched during this period.

The afternoon after the shoe shiner was taken into protective custody, one of Tulsa's more sensationalist newspapers published a story about the incident, of course being careful to only state the facts. No wait, that's not right, they actually made it sound like the shoe shiner raped the elevator operator and threw in an editorial stating that the shoe shiner was most definitely going to get lynched. You can probably guess what happened next. Within a few hours of the paper being published, a lynch mob of several hundred people showed up at the courthouse. This did not sit well with the Black population of Greenwood, and after some debate, some 30 young men armed themselves and went to the courthouse to support the besieged police. Tensions rose on both sides, with several people firing guns in the air to show how serious they were, which quickly shifted into firing guns into each other. When the smoke cleared, ten White men and two Black men were dead. The shock of the sudden violence quickly gave way to a full on riot, with armed Whites chasing Blacks in a running gun battle through the streets.

Rumors quickly began circulating throughout Tulsa that a full on race revolution was occurring. Thousands of White people armed themselves and surrounded the Greenwood neighborhood, where the local Black populace prepared to defend their homes and businesses. Both sides took pot shots at each other throughout the night. The Oklahoma National Guard was quickly deployed, but they did little to stop the violence, instead setting themselves up in defensive positions around the edge of the Greenwood neighborhood. Seeing no chance of protection from the authorities, many Black people began to flee the city. The following morning, the White rioters, many of whom had military training, launched a full on assault on Greenwood. Masses of White men marched up the streets, shooting indiscriminately, lighting buildings on fire, and even hanging some Black residents. Several of the rioters, some of them possibly police officers, commandeered biplanes from the local airport, which they used to drop homemade firebombs on the neighborhood. Attempts by the fire department to fight the fires were stopped by the rioters. The Oklahoma National Guard troops, bolstered by reinforcements, finally took action to end the riot by midday. By that time, some 300 people had been killed (around 250 Black and 50 White), 800 wounded, and 35 city blocks had been burned, leaving 10,000 African-Americans homeless. Some 6,000 members of the Black community who had not fled, were rounded up and held en masse at three internment centers for several days.

Most of the residents of Greenwood spent close to a year in tents as they tried to rebuild their neighborhood, a process greatly lengthened by attempts by city leaders to halt construction via new stringent building codes and re-zoning efforts. Though Greenwood was eventually rebuilt, it never reclaimed its former glory, becoming a slum during the Great Depression and eventually being mostly torn down for a new freeway during the 1970's. Though some 85 people were indicted for their participation in the riot, none were ever convicted. The incident was collectively forgotten and scrubbed from the city's historical record. City officials didn't formally apologize until the 1990's.

#19 Rinderpest

Aside from North and South America, few other continents have gotten such a raw deal from contact with their neighbors quite as much as Africa. Throughout most of history, Africa was seen mostly as a source of exotic trade goods and slaves. However, people from Europe and the Middle East mostly stayed on the coast, avoiding the interior with the exception of South Africa. This was largely due to the fact that the interior of Africa was completely chock full of deadly tropical diseases and well armed and organized tribes and kingdoms, who were less than welcoming to those daring to venture inland. However, as the European powers began to jockey for actual control of Africa's resources, things quickly got out of hand.

In the 1880's, Italy just up and decided one day that it would be in its best interest to control the areas of the region known as the Horn of Africa. The only problem with this idea was that the various peoples living there, most notably the Ethiopians, were not really down with the whole idea. Things got rather violent. It was during these various campaigns, around 1889, that the Italian army got the bright idea that they should totally ship in some cattle from India and the Middle East to help feed its troops. Unfortunately, these cattle were infected by a nasty air borne disease known as rinderpest, which though common in the homeland of the cattle, had never been seen before in Africa. You can probably guess what happened next. The disease spread rapidly amongst the cattle, goats, sheep, and oxen of the locals, killing some 90 percent within a few years. This was not exactly a good thing for the locals, who not only depended on their cattle for food, but also their oxen for plowing their fields. While many people reverted to farming by hand, things only got worse when a drought swept the area. By the end of the epidemic, an estimated third of the population of Ethiopia had starved to death. Things just got shittier from there.

To the south of Ethiopia were the famed savannas of Kenya and Tanzania, home to numerous nomadic tribes, the most powerful of whom were the Maasai. Most of these tribes, the Maasai chief amongst them, were entirely dependent upon their large cattle herds for sustenance. With cattle theft a common practice, some unlucky bastards stole some cattle from Ethiopia. It was a major mistake. Within months, millions of cattle were dead and dying, removing the only source of food for the Maasai and the other tribes. Within a few years, an estimated two-thirds of the Maasai starved to death. The sheer number of cattle and people dying horrified the European powers who controlled the coast, but not to the degree that it kept them from moving into the interior to take control of the territory that the Maasai were no longer able to defend. In the meanwhile, the rinderpest outbreak continued making its way south, eventually crossing the Zambeze River and threatening British controlled South Africa. Not really down with 90 percent of their cattle dying, the British carried out various schemes to halt the spread of the virus. The first attempt was to build a thousand mile barbed wire fence. This worked about as well as you would imagine it would. The next strategy was to kill every susceptible animal in a zone several hundred miles wide stretching across the continent. People used to think big back then. This worked to the degree that it slowed the disease, but still millions of cattle in South Africa died before the epidemic burned itself out around the end of the century.

If all of this sounds pretty horrorific, then it might not be a good time to mention that things weren't over yet. The rinderpest epidemic not only killed 90 percent of the cattle in East Africa, it also killed around 50 percent of the various wild cloven hooved animals; such as wildebeest, giraffes, and various types of antelope. The resulting depopulation of grazing animals resulted in wide areas of the savanna shifting from grasslands to large swaths of scrubby thorn bushes. These areas were the perfect breeding ground for tsetse flies, a blood sucking bastard who also happened to be the primary carrier of sleeping sickness, a terrible disease which drives people insane, makes them extremely lethargic, and then finally kills them. Though tsetse flies had always been in Africa, the greatly boosted population caused a sleeping sickness outbreak across Eastern Africa from 1901 through 1908 which killed hundreds of thousands of people, including up to two thirds of the native population in some regions. This pretty much ended any native attempts to stop the European colonial takeover.

The Europeans who took control of the savannas mostly concentrated on creating large plantations and ranches, as well as giant game preserves. The truth of the matter was that the Europeans were more horrified by the deaths of so many big game animals rather than the fate of all the people that had died. After all, while a bunch of so-called savages perishing was one thing, it was nothing compared to not being able to go big game hunting. So yeah, it was that kind of fucked up. A combination of these game preserves, a ban on any natives killing wild animals, and large swaths of tsetse infested scrubland being avoided, and therefore undeveloped, led to an explosion in wild animal populations to levels likely higher than before the outbreak. This included lions, which led to a sharp increase in the number of lion attacks on villages, which the locals were pretty much just told to shut up and get used to. Some modern ecologists would later say that the rinderpest outbreak was the greatest boon to African wildlife in modern history, which though true, is still probably a shitty thing to say all things considered. Research into both sleeping sickness and rinderpest resulted in the development of effective quarantine and treatment methods by World War II, though outbreaks still periodically occurred. Rinderpest was declared globally eradicated in 2010. Sleeping sickness still kills 3,500 people in Africa each year.

#20 Comic Books

In the early 1930's, a printing press company specializing in color printing was facing a bit of an issue. Due to a little thing known as the Great Depression, pretty much everybody in the entirety of the United States was a little strapped for cash. As a result, most newspapers and businesses did away with anything luxurious or frivolous, with color printing being top of the list. Not really wanting to just call it a day and declare bankruptcy, the printing company instead came up with a desperate scheme which involved putting all the old newspaper comic strips they could find in a single big book and selling it for dirt cheap. The collection actually sold amazingly well, and so was born the comic book.

Now being business people, the owners of this printing press of course squeezed their new cash cow as much as humanely possible by going into overdrive printing new collections. However, there was just one little problem, they quickly ran out of already printed comic strips. Not wanting to go back to worrying about not making money, the printers instead got the bright idea that they should just make up their own original comics. This worked quite well, and before you could say Jack's your uncle, or whatever the hell it was old timey people said, numerous competitors were jumping into the new industry. Now unlike a newspaper, having a whole book to fill opened up a lot of opportunities for would be writers and artists. Where once comics were limited to short strips, suddenly it was possible to do lengthier features. What once was once an art form dominated by puns expanded into a mode of storytelling with complete, and at times complex, plots. Nearly every genre had its own comic book, with the most popular being horror, crime, science fiction, westerns, romance, and superheroes. By the 1940's, comic books were read by nearly everybody in the country.

Things went pretty well for the comics industry until the 1950's, a time when people who got home from a war that was supposedly fought for freedom began to wonder if perhaps they were starting to get way too much freedom back home. The war against comic books began when a crackpot psychologist, who apparently really hated comics, wrote a popular book claiming that they were turning children into violent homoerotic sociopaths. People being the way they have always been, many freaked right the fuck out, leading to a growing movement to outlaw comics and even a hearing before the U.S. Senate. As a result, the comics industry freaked right the fuck out too, and soon after they created what became known as the Comics Code Authority, which forcefully censored the industry by using public worry to guarantee that newsstands and other distributors would only carry comics that had the CCA's seal of approval. The CCA completely banned the showing of violence, gore, and overt sexuality. However, it also banned anything that questioned people in authority or the two point three kids and a big slice of apple pie version of American values. It should be pretty obvious that this was pretty much all of the good stuff, and as a result, comic book readership plummeted, and many companies went out of business. By the mid-1960's, the only people still widely reading comics were adolescent boys, resulting in a greater concentration on titles focused on children's humor and superheroes.

As mainstream comic book companies increasingly focused on the saccharin laced and American flag waving story lines required by the CCA, other comic book artists went underground to circumvent the censorship. Creatively called the 'underground comics scene', these artists created heavily sexualized satirical characters who subverted authority and questioned everything and anything being declared normal at the time. These comics were mostly sold via unconventional distributors, such as head shops, and by the late 1960's had become popular on many college campuses as part of the counterculture. The growing competition of the underground scene, led to many mainstream artists working within the code to push its boundaries, which in turn started to force changes to the code, such as allowing corrupt public officials in comics, but only if they got their comeuppance. This marked the beginning of the end for the CCA and its censorship.

In 1971, the U.S. government approached Marvel Comics to create a superhero comic about drug abuse. While pretty standard stuff these days, at the time it was a fairly novel request, especially given the fact that the depiction of drug use was totally against the code. Though the CCA refused to give the comic its seal of approval, Marvel printed it anyways, figuring the U.S. government was a bit of a bigger deal than the CCA. Marvel was absolutely right, the comic was a major hit, and the CCA was shown to be the toothless bully it had always been. However, though the CCA was shown to be nothing but a boogey man, it continued to at least try to give the illusion that it had control for several decades more. The CCA stamp was common on most comics clear through the 1990's, even though everything the code was supposedly against slowly became more commonplace throughout the industry. The CCA finally became fully defunct in 2011. As a result, comic books have made a comeback in recent years, with stories branching out from the old muscly people in tights plots to stories in about every genre you can think of, attracting readers of all ages. You can find these resurgent comic books in about every bookstore and library in the country, only now we call them graphic novels.

#21 Lend Me An Ear

In 1888, Paul Gauguin was a struggling forty year old painter who mostly survived by taking menial jobs and figuring out ways to scam government assistance programs. A former wealthy stockbroker and arts dealer, Paul had lost pretty much all of his money during a bad economic downturn a few years before. For whatever reason, this experience made Paul decide that he should totally be a full time artist, much to the chagrin of his Danish wife, who was left to be the sole breadwinner for the family. Not really being down with a grown man just moping around the house, Paul's wife suggested that if he wanted to be a painter he should totally just go to Paris, probably figuring it was better to have him gone. After all, the woman had five children to raise, she didn't need a sixth. Paul, happy as a clam at the suggestion, did just that.

Things were not easy for Paul in Paris, home to pretty much all struggling artists in the late-nineteenth century. Though he had managed to sell some paintings, by all appearances he was doomed to flounder about in obscurity. However, his luck finally changed when quite by a chance a man saw some of Paul's paintings at a small gallery. Falling completely head over heels for the paintings, the man declared that Paul was one of the finest painters in the world and convinced his brother, a well known art dealer, to purchase several of them and hang them at the brother's posh art gallery. This was quite a big break for Paul, since thanks to the well-known art dealer his work would finally be seen by a wealthier class of clientele. The name of the art dealer was Theo van Gogh, and the name of the brother was Vincent. Yeah, you can probably guess where this is going to go.

By 1888, Vincent was a struggling 35 year old artist who mostly survived thanks to the financial help of his brother Theo, who for some reason loved Vincent more than anything in the world despite the fact that Vincent was often times nuttier than a pile of squirrel shit. Vincent was known for manic episodes, during which he would create hundreds of paintings to the detriment of his health, surviving mostly on alcohol and pipe tobacco, and forgetting to eat to the point that his teeth would start to loosen. Vincent was also known for his passions. For a time he had wanted to be a priest, but he had given it up in favor of stalking his cousin to the point that his family had to stage an intervention, to which he responded by lighting his arm on fire and then living with a prostitute for close to a year. The two brothers then lived together for a time, until Vincent got thrown out of art school and became such a pain in the ass that Theo bought him a house in the town of Arles, 465 miles from Paris.

Anyways, when Paul Gauguin came into the picture, Vincent was all hot and heavy for his new idea of starting an art commune. Completely enraptured by Paul, Vincent convinced his brother Theo to convince Paul to move in with him. While less than enthusiastic about the idea of moving in with someone with severe mental issues, Paul eventually relented, giving in on the promise of free rent and the implied threat of Theo no longer displaying Paul's work. Amazingly enough, things started out pretty fine. The two men got along well, sharing a studio, painting each others' portraits, and visiting local brothels together. However, that only lasted a few weeks. It's hard to say exactly when things went wrong, but it probably had something to do with the notoriously dickish Paul being rude about Vincent's art. Vincent, who thought Paul was his new BFF, responded by see-sawing wildly between super clingy and out of his mind angry. Paul would often awaken in the middle of the night to find Vincent watching him sleep, and Vincent once threw a glass at Paul's head, to which Paul responded by threatening to strangle Vincent in his sleep.

After nine weeks, Paul decided that enough was enough. On an appropriately dramatic rainy day, he packed his bags to move back to Paris. Vincent, watching his dreams of a commune collapse right before his eyes, went after his former friend with a straight razor. After Paul left in a bit of a hurry, Vincent decided he might as well kick things up a notch. He used the razor to cut off his ear, and then walked down to the brothel to give it to his favorite prostitute. This whole episode was a little much for Theo, who had his brother committed. Vincent would be in and out of asylums for the rest of his life, which wasn't long since he shot himself a year and a half later. Theo, missing his brother terribly, went crazy and died six months later. As for Paul, being the classiest of dudes, he traveled to Tahiti, where he spent his time painting and fucking 14 year old local girls, some of which he impregnated, and all of which he gave syphilis. Paul lived out the rest of his total shitbag life in a thatched hut he called the House of Orgasms, dying of a likely opium overdose at the age of 54. Neither Paul or Vincent became famous artists until after their deaths, but their lives did inspire a lot of future aspiring artists to be as crazy and/or shitty of people as possible.

#22 Real Estate and Blue Dresses Part 1

On January 20, 1993, Bill Clinton was inaugurated the 42nd president of the United States and probably almost immediately began to partially wish that he had never taken the job. A resurgent Republican delegation in Congress, led by Representative Newt Gingrich, unhappy with losing the presidency for the first time in twelve years, was all sorts of hot and heavy about knocking Clinton down a notch or two. To their way of thinking, Clinton was a political outsider who had all sorts of questionable skeletons in his closet. The Clinton administration did little to dispel this notion. Within months of taking power, the general bungling of several key Clinton officials caused a multitude of scandals, leading to the Republicans calling for and getting a multitude of investigations, to which the administration responded by being as completely unhelpful as humanly possible. It was a completely ridiculous shit show on all sides of the equation. One of the largest and most remembered of these investigations was Whitewater.

In the 1980's, Bill and Hillary Clinton and their shifty as shit friends Jim and Susan McDougal invested in a real estate venture called Whitewater. The McDougals were long time associates of the Clintons. Jim McDougal often held fundraisers to help Bill's political career and he also retained the services of the Rose Law Firm, of which Hillary Clinton was a partner. Unfortunately, the deal didn't quite work out, leading to a desperate Jim McDougal trying to cover the partnership's losses via an illegal government loan to his wife, which he coerced out of another shifty as shit associate named David Hale. The loan failed to save Whitewater, but this was just one of many shady deals that Jim McDougal was involved in, pretty much all of them including convoluted and illegal loans from a bank owned by Jim to various shady folks and ventures. Jim's bank eventually went insolvent in 1989, mostly due to the sheer volume of crazy/illegal schemes, which promptly resulted in a wide ranging investigation.

While all of this was going on, Bill Clinton did quite well for himself, serving first as the governor of Arkansas and then getting himself elected president. Aside from some brief headlines during the Democratic primaries, Whitewater was not even mentioned during the campaign. However, the investigation into Jim McDougal's failed bank kept chugging right along, eventually resulting in a referral to the Justice Department in the fall of 1992. The referral stated the need for a criminal investigation against the McDougals and naming the Clintons as possible witnesses and/or beneficiaries of illegal actions. The referral pretty much just sat ignored on a desk for a year, causing the investigators to send a second referral in the fall of 1993. The Justice Department responded to this second referral by reviewing and rejecting the first referral, declaring it to be without merit.

Some people must not have been too happy with this chain of events, because soon after news of the rejection leaked to the press. This raised some eyebrows since several of the rejecting officials had close ties to the Clintons, chief amongst them Webster Hubbell, who had worked with Hillary in the Rose Law Firm. The eyebrows went even higher when David Hale, recently indicted for a completely unrelated charge of insurance fraud, publicly claimed that Bill Clinton had used his position as governor to coerce Hale into giving Susan McDougal the illegal loan to try and save Whitewater. The Republicans went wild, screaming about a possible cover up. At first the Democrats called it a bunch of malarkey, but then the press struck again. Earlier that summer, the Deputy White House Counsel, Vince Foster, had committed suicide, after which members of the White House staff had blocked investigators from entering his office for two days, during which time sources claimed a large number of Whitewater and other legal files had been removed. The news overwhelmed what resistance the Democrats could muster, and at the start of 1994, Robert Fiske, a private attorney, was appointed special counsel to investigate.

Robert Fiske pretty much sat right in a shit sandwich and pretty quickly got in over his head. Though a subpoena had resulted in the Whitewater files from Foster's office being handed over by the Clintons' personal lawyers, rumors were claiming that the documents had been in the possession of the Clintons themselves for several days. An idea which in turn sparked speculation that Vince Foster had actually been murdered. Not having many leads, Fiske chose to focus on claims that Webster Hubbell had illegally alerted the Clintons of the criminal referrals to the Justice Department. Hubbell had only just been recently indicted for unrelated charges of embezzlement, and it was hoped that a deal could be struck. However, Hubbell adamantly refused to have anything to do with the special prosecutor. After six months of lackluster investigation, Fiske released his report which concluded that Foster's death was a suicide, the same conclusion of the police and FBI, and that there was no proof of the White House interfering with any investigation regarding Whitewater or the McDougals. However, things were far from over.

Stuff You Should Know

#23 Real Estate and Blue Dresses Part 2

The same day special counsel Robert Fiske released his report, President Clinton signed into law a bill to reauthorize the use of independent counsels, which had first been created after the whole Nixon-Watergate shitshow. The difference was that while special counsels were named by the Attorney General, an independent counsel was appointed by a panel of judges. The change in the law saw the ousting of Fiske and the appointment of Ken Starr, a former Solicitor General and one time candidate for the Supreme Court. Where Fiske had been rather lukewarm as an investigator, Starr was if anything overzealous. Upon taking up the position, Starr did away with all of Fiske's conclusions, even re-opening the investigation into whether or not Vince Foster had committed suicide, even though the police stated that he mostly certainly had killed himself.

Right before the appointment of Starr, news of a leak to the media forced the White House to admit that Foster's legal documents had been kept in their personal residence for five days before being handed over to the Clintons' personal lawyer. This was pretty big news considering that a number of documents, mostly related to Hillary's time working as legal counsel for Jim McDougal's bank, were reported to be missing from those handed over to investigators. Unlike his predecessor, Starr saw Jim McDougal and his convoluted loans as the main avenue to proving any wrongdoing. Targeting various people in Arkansas who had worked with McDougal, he began building a case which he hoped would force both Jim and Sue McDougal, who had since divorced, to turn state's evidence and support David Hale's claims that Bill Clinton used his political power as governor to solicit and coerce favors beneficial to his personal and campaign finances. Within a little over half a year, Starr managed to get four people to plead guilty on various charges and to agree to cooperate with the investigation on the promise of lesser charges. One of these was a banker who admitted to embezzling funds for Clinton's political campaign, though no proof that the president knew about it could be found. Another was Webster Hubbell, though he proved to be less cooperative than he had promised in his plea deal.

While Starr went after McDougal's associates, the Republicans surged in the 1994 election, giving them control of the House of Representatives and Senate for the first time since 1955. Both the newly Republican House and Senate soon after launched new investigations into

50

Whitewater and other scandals, not trusting the results of Democratic Congressional led investigations the previous year. The investigations quickly broke down into partisan bickering, but they did manage to keep Whitewater in the news cycle. As political hissing filled the news, Starr continued his investigation, indicting Jim and Sue McDougal for bank fraud in August of 1995. Starr's ultimate goal was to force the Clintons to testify as witnesses in the McDougal cases, which would create on the record testimony which could lead to possible charges of perjury if it was proven that they were lying. However, legal wrangling on whether or not the president could be called as a witness slowed everything down. This stalemate ended in April of 1996, with the president forced by a court order to testify. A month later, both McDougals were convicted. Soon after, the president was forced to testify again in July, this time in the trial of two of Jim McDougal's associates.

During this same period, Hillary was running into her own problems. Under increasing pressure, she finally produced the missing documents pertaining to her time with the Rose Law Firm, claiming that apparently they had just been sitting on an end table in the White House the whole time. This strange claim resulted in her being subpoenaed by Starr, the first time a First Lady had ever been subpoenaed. Starr felt like he was getting close. Though both Clintons continued to swear complete ignorance of the doings of their associates, both were now liable for perjury if it could be proven.

With both McDougals convicted, but still waiting to be sentenced, Starr offered leniency in return for testimony. Jim McDougal turned almost immediately, making grand claims that both Clintons had been involved in various schemes that benefited them both directly and indirectly. He also claimed that he had been offered a pardon to keep his mouth shut. Unfortunately, Jim McDougal was far from the perfect witness. Aside from making many erratic and contradictory statements, none of his claims could be fully connected to the ones earlier made by Hale. This left Sue McDougal as the key to Starr's case, since her testimony could verify that of her ex-husbands. However, Sue McDougal proved to be a harder nut to crack. Not only did she refuse to testify, but also publicly claimed that Jim had told her to lie about the Clintons to get a more lenient sentence. In an attempt to break Sue McDougal, Starr stacked more charges against her and had her transferred from one prison to another for over a year. None of it worked.

As time dragged on, public interest in the Whitewater case began to wane. The whole thing was complicated as hell with all sorts of strange legal nuances which did little to capture the public imagination. In November of 1996, Bill Clinton was elected president for a second term. In April of 1997, facing imminent news reports, the White House was forced to admit that aides had funneled money to the defense fund of Webster Hubbell. Despite this, Starr's investigation continued to lose steam throughout the rest of the year. Sue McDougal either would not break or was telling the truth. Though Starr drafted an impeachment referral that fall, he never released it. Instead he only announced that investigations had shown that Vince Foster had most definitely committed suicide. In March of 1998, Jim McDougal died in prison of a heart attack. The Whitewater investigation was dead in the water, but it didn't matter, Starr was making one last ditch effort in a different direction.

#24 Real Estate and Blue Dresses Part 3

In May of 1994, a 28 year old woman by the name of Paula Jones filed a lawsuit against sitting president Bill Clinton, claiming that he had pulled out his dick and stroked it in front of her three years prior when he was governor. The charge came a few months after a pair of Arkansas State Troopers claimed that they had helped the president find random women to fuck, citing the first name of one such woman as Paula. The Jones lawsuit quickly became mired down in legal mumbo jumbo. Clinton attempted to claim presidential immunity, meaning that the case wouldn't be allowed to proceed until he was no longer president, a maneuver that delayed the case for years as it worked its way through the court system. In May of 1997, the Supreme Court ruled unanimously that the court case could proceed. Throughout this period, Jones' lawyers had her hitting the news and talk show circuit in hopes of getting more women to come forward. The lawyers hoped to establish a pattern of impropriety to help prove Jones' claim. While no victims chose to come forward at the time, someone did leave an anonymous tip about a woman they should talk to. That woman was Monica Lewinsky.

In 1997, Monica Lewinsky was a 24 year old Pentagon employee who for a ten month period between 1995 and 1996 had worked as a White House intern. During this period, she began an affair with the president that involved blowjobs and putting cigars in places where cigars probably shouldn't go. Worried about such behavior, the White House staff had Lewinsky transferred to the Pentagon, but the affair continued off and on. When Lewinsky was subpoenaed by the Jones case in January of 1998, she testified that no such affair had occurred. Within days, a so-called friend and confidante of Lewinsky's, named Linda Tripp, approached Independent Counsel Ken Starr with over twenty hours of secretly taped conversations with Lewinsky talking about the affair, including claims that the president had asked Lewinsky to lie under oath.

It should go without saying that such news got Starr all sorts of hot and bothered. Working fast, he got permission from a judiciary panel to look into the matter, and then waited for Clinton to testify in the Jones case a few days later. In his testimony, the president denied having an affair with Lewinsky. For the beleaguered Ken Starr, facing a failing Whitewater investigation, it was a godsend. As news of the affair began getting leaked to the press, three more women came forward claiming that they had at one time or another been groped by Bill Clinton. Another woman would come forward a year later, claiming that Clinton had raped her. The president denied all of it, basically calling Lewinsky a lying slut, and his wife Hillary proclaimed a whole thing a massive right wing conspiracy. Over a six month period, Starr negotiated with Lewinsky in an attempt to get her to admit the truth, during which time she did a modeling spread for Vogue magazine. In July, she made a deal to testify in return for immunity, sweetening the deal by handing over a blue dress with a presidential cum stain. She soon after testified before a grand jury.

Ken Starr was undoubtedly enjoying the whole thing. President Clinton, facing insurmountable evidence, was subpoenaed by the grand jury and forced to testify that he had indeed had an affair. However, he refused to admit that he had lied under oath in the Jones case, claiming he did not consider a blowjob sex and arguing over the definition of the word 'is'. Soon after, the independent counsel released his Starr Report, which contained every lurid detail of the Lewinsky affair, to the House of Representatives and to the public, calling for impeachment on the basis of perjury and obstruction of justice. The Judiciary Committee of the House began impeachment proceedings soon after, which stretched over the next several months. A period Clinton used to settle the Jones case out of court, Starr used to announce the Whitewater investigation as inconclusive, and Hustler magazine used to pay a bounty for proof of infidelity by any member of Congress. Due to Hustlers efforts, several Republicans were forced to resign, one of them being both Speaker of the House Newt Gingrich and his replacement as speaker.

In December of 1998, the Judiciary Committee passed articles of impeachment and the matter moved on to the full House. Though the vote was delayed by the president calling airstrikes on Iraq, a mission actually planned months earlier, the Republican led House voted to impeach President Clinton. The impeachment trial began in the Senate in January of 1999. After a month and a half of testimony and debate, the Republican majority Senate failed to meet the two-thirds vote required for impeachment. Many felt that lying about where you put your dick just wasn't a good enough reason to declare somebody to be unfit to be president. Bill Clinton served out the remainder of his second term.

Ken Starr continued to pursue the Watergate investigation until late 1999, when he stepped down and was replaced by a federal prosecutor named Robert Ray. Under direction to wrap things up, Robert Ray announced in 2000 that there was not enough evidence to pursue a charge of wrongdoing by either Bill or Hillary Clinton in relation to any of the accusations. In total, 15 associates of the Clintons were convicted of over 40 crimes; including fraud, embezzlement, and conspiracy. In November of 2000, Hillary Clinton won a Senate seat in New York, launching her own political career. As for Bill, likely facing charges of perjury in relation to the Jones case as soon as he left office, he made a deal with Ray on his second to last day, agreeing to admit to making false statements in return for surrendering his law license. The next day he pardoned four of the people convicted by the investigation, including Susan McDougal.

#25 Posture

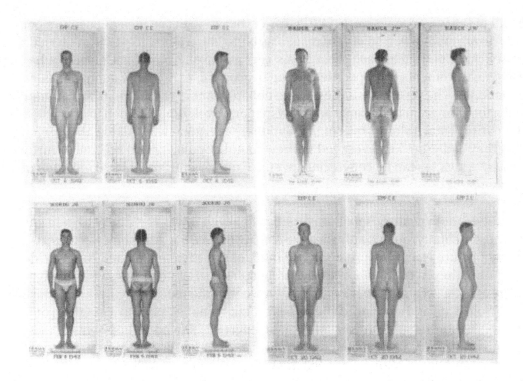

Professor William Sheldon was a man of his time, by which I of course mean he was a sexist racist who did considerable study in the field of eugenics. Starting in the 1930's, Sheldon developed a strange theory, called somatotyping, that physical measurements could be used to determine an individual's character. He divided human beings into three extremes; skinny and nervous ectomorphs, fat and jolly endomorphs, and confident and buffed mesomorphs; and hypothesized that not only did all people express these extremes to one degree or another, but that these ratios could be measured using a three digit number which would reveal someone's personality. If this all sounds like a bunch of garbage to you, then good, because it is. However, at the time, such theories, rigorously pursued by flawed uses of the scientific method, were given a large amount of credence.

In order to prove his theory, Sheldon of course needed to examine and measure a large number of naked people. Luckily for him, he was not the only scientist interested in measuring naked bodies. Since as early as the 1880's, Harvard University, then a men's only institution, had been doing posture studies on its students, by which I mean they were coercing many of them to have naked photographs taken for various somatological studies. Sheldon used these photographs, along with measurements taken at nearby outpatient clinics, to create two major studies linking physique and temperament, which were released in the early 1940's. The studies were met with a great amount of interest, because at the time anything declaring ways you could scientifically prove you were better than other people was of interest. However, further research was curtailed by a little thing called World War II, during which Sheldon worked in the medical corp.

By the end of the war, people were a little less enthused with the idea of eugenics, for reasons. However, Sheldon's work was seen as being different since it wasn't based on nationality. After getting himself setup at a sweet ass lab at Columbia University, he began collecting measurements from people visiting nearby clinics, juvenile delinquents, and mental patients. The resulting studies, while debated amongst the scientific community, received a lot of press in magazines and newspapers, exploding Sheldon and his theories onto the national stage almost overnight. Suddenly everyone was talking about what types of bodies they had. Sheldon leveraged his new found popularity and acclaim to further his research, by which I mean he convinced dozens of universities to start taking nude photos of their students.

In the mid-twentieth century, most universities believed it was their duty to help students excel not just mentally, but also physically. As part of this, most freshman students underwent posture exams, where doctors would look at them naked and then decide whether or not they needed to be enrolled in posture correcting programs. Taking advantage of these existing programs, Sheldon went to the men's only Ivy League schools (Harvard, Yale, etc.) and convinced them to start taking naked photos from the front, side, and rear for his studies. The universities readily agreed. Sheldon's hope was to use the photographs and measurements to create what he called an Atlas of Men. Of course if he was going to have an Atlas of Men, he needed an Atlas of Women as well, so soon after he also convinced the women's only Seven Sisters (Vassar, Smith, etc.) to start taking naked posture photographs as well. Again, the university leaders were totally okay with all of this. From there he convinced half a dozen Midwestern universities to join the fun.

The strange thing about all of this was how quickly it became normalized. Aside from threats of a lawsuit in Seattle when Sheldon tried to spread the practice to the West Coast, everyone just kind of went along with the idea that it was perfectly normal for prestigious schools to take nude photographs of incoming freshman. The practice continued throughout the 1950's and 1960's, with some of those photographed later becoming famous business people, politicians, actors, and other such folk of note. It wasn't until rumors began to spread that some of the photographs, mostly women, were ending up in the hands of the non-scientific types that protests began, leading to the practice being ended completely by the early 1970's. It probably didn't hurt that by then Sheldon's theories had largely been debunked.

Under public pressure from those whose photographs were taken, many who had become powerful people, most of the posture photographs were burned to make sure they never got out to the public. However, even into the 1990's, caches of the pictures were still being discovered in random drawers and boxes. A significant collection even found its way to the Smithsonian, though much of that collection was believed to have been burned by 2005. Though Sheldon's broader theories have largely been debunked, the methods he created for measuring body shape remain widely used in science to this day.

#26 Pinball Wizard

In 1920, the United States passed the Eighteenth Amendment, effectively banning the production and sale of alcohol nationwide. This of course made the drinking of alcohol cool as all get out, and as a result a bunch of people became willing to pay out the nose to get their hands on some sweet sweet booze. If you have any sense of history whatsoever you probably already know what happened next, but for the ignorant bastards amongst you, I'll go ahead and just say it. Prohibition led directly to the rise of organized crime. Local thugs, who once made their living shaking down local small business owners, suddenly found themselves raking in obscene amounts of dough from black market liquor sales, some of which they used to bribe local officials and to buy firearms to use on their competition. However, the whole shebang came crashing down in 1933 when the government, realizing that they could be the crooks making money off of booze, ended Prohibition.

It should probably go without saying that the end of Prohibition was not seen as a good thing by organized crime. With a good chunk of their income suddenly gone, the gangsters were forced to increasingly rely upon their other sources of illicit funds, the largest being illegal gambling. The most popular of such games of chance were slot machines, mostly because they were easy to move around, didn't take many people to oversee or maintain, and could be easily rigged. During Prohibition, slot machines were seen as pretty low level crimes, but the legalization of booze quickly changed that. Vice cops who wanted to keep their jobs, and politicians who still wanted to be seen as tough on crime, shifted their focus to wiping slot machines off the map, destroying thousands over the next several years. That's when the entrepreneurial criminals got creative.

In 1931, some dude named David Gottlieb invented what we today call the pinball machine. The early pinball machines were similar to the modern version in that they involved shooting a ball via a spring loaded plunger. However, they lacked flippers to keep the ball in play. Pinball proved to be extremely popular, both amongst adults and children, with machines quickly popping up across the country in bars, drug stores, and other such places. Hundreds of companies started manufacturing the machines, which collectively around the country made more money a year than the entire motion picture industry. However, though many were owned by legitimate businesses, the pinball machine turned out to be a godsend to organized crime. While slot machines were being increasingly targeted, purveyors of illegal games of chance shifted to pinball machines to make up the difference, turning them into a form of gambling by promising payouts if players reached certain scores.

The politicians and vice squads of the day were of course not blind to such shenanigans, but it was difficult to prove whether or not a pinball machine was being used for gambling or just for fun. This left the enforcers of law in a bit of a quandary, which they eventually solved by calling for the outright ban of the machines. In 1942, buoyed by claims that pinball was teaching children to gamble, New York City became the first major city to outlaw pinball. Over the next decade, almost every major city in the country followed suit. Thousands of machines were seized and destroyed.

Despite such setbacks, the pinball industry continued to stagger onward over the next several decades. Organized crime moved on, shifting their focus to legal gambling in Las Vegas and eventually illegal drugs, but low-level crooks continued to run illegal pinball machines in various bars and other locations. Many of these were ignored by police, what with other actual crimes occurring, though the occasional raid or palm greasing still took place. For their part, the pinball manufacturers tried to distance themselves from the idea that the machines were games of chance by introducing more features requiring skill, including the addition of flippers in 1947. However, the stigma proved hard to remove. Throughout the 1950's and most of the 1960's, various media used the playing of pinball as shorthand for the rebelliousness of youth.

The ban on pinball machines didn't start to end until 1976, when a pinball wizard named Roger Sharpe proved to the New York City Council that it was a game of skill by calling his shots. The ban was soon after ended in most other cities, though some bans remained on the books as late as 2016. Suddenly legal, pinball entered a new heyday which came to an abrupt end as video game arcades became popular in the 1980's. Eventually the industry collapsed to only a single manufacturer, though it has found new popularity again in recent years.

#27 Chinese Takeout

In 1849, gold was discovered in California and a ridiculously large number of people collectively lost their shit. Dreaming of future riches, tens of thousands of these people packed their bags and headed west in hopes of just scooping a fortune out of the water. Unfortunately, as is often the case with such things, few of them actually got rich. The easily claimed gold was quickly snatched up, leaving the majority of the gold to be mined via industrial methods that cost a lot of money to set up. These industrial mining methods were fairly labor intensive, but the majority of American emigrants were not really into doing back breaking labor for shit wages. They much preferred staking land claims. This left the mine owners with one of two options, either they could raise wages, or they could find other sources of labor. You can probably guess which one they picked.

The 1850's in China was not really that great of a time to be alive, the nation was embroiled in a civil war called the Taiping Rebellion, which thanks to both sides using the strategy of just killing every poor fucker they could, was one of the bloodiest wars in world history. Even areas not directly affected by the war faced economic collapse due to the chaos. This is probably why so many Chinese jumped at the sudden chance of going to America, because after all, shitty wages for doing a shitty job was still better than no wages at all. Most of the Chinese who came to America were men, who planned on working for a while before returning home. Though initially working in the mines, they quickly spread to many other shitty low paying jobs, such as building railroads. Of course, this being nineteenth century America, they faced a shit ton of racism for the horrible crime of looking slightly different. This wasn't helped by the fact that all Chinese men at the time were required by Chinese law to keep their hair in a super long braid called a queue. If a Chinese man cut off his queue, he would be beheaded upon returning home to China, which probably goes a long way towards explaining why the country was in the middle of a civil war.

Things pretty much went along this way until the 1870's, when the economies of the United States and Europe entered a severe recession that lasted most of the decade. People who had once thought many shitty jobs to be beneath them, suddenly started getting all riled up about a bunch of foreigners stealing jobs from hardworking Americans. To their way of thinking, the jobs wouldn't be so shitty if they paid better, but the owners had no reason to raise wages as long as they had access to cheap Chinese labor. As a result, emerging labor unions and random folks who just got off on being racist fucks doubled down on treating the Chinese like shit, up to and including random murders. Eventually, a bunch of super racist laws were passed making it more difficult for the Chinese to find work, culminating in the Exclusion Act of 1882 which just straight up made Chinese immigration illegal. The Chinese already in the U.S. were caught between a rock and a hard place. On the one hand, even though they were treated like shit there were still greater opportunities for them in America, on the other, under the new law if they went home to visit China they would be unable to return to the U.S. Though thousands chose to return to China over the next several decades, many decided to remain. Since labor union violence and racist laws barred them from many jobs, they formed close knit communities in many large cities on the west and east coast, running low margin businesses such as laundries

This is pretty much how things remained until a decision by a federal court created a loophole in the Exclusion Act. Under the act, Chinese merchants were allowed to return to China and bring back workers if they owned certain businesses, though few Chinese owned the businesses were included on the list. That changed in 1915, when a federal court order added restaurants to the list, though they had to be high end restaurants, which was defined as the owner not doing menial labor. To take advantage, groups of Chinese pooled their money to open restaurants, which allowed them to get visas to bring their family and friends to the U.S. To get around the owner not doing menial work rule, the Chinese would take turns being the boss, each fulfilling the year long requirement needed to get their merchant visa. Those brought to America would save their money to open their own restaurants, which would then give them the opportunity to bring in even more people. A second obstacle was the requirement that the visas be signed by a White witness who was willing to vouch that no shenanigans were going on. To get around this, the Chinese restaurateurs made deals with shady food vendors who were willing to give signatures in exchange for exclusive contracts. This raised the prices the restaurants had to pay for ingredients, which forced the Chinese to change their recipes to use cheaper alternatives, thus creating many of the so-called Chinese dishes so many Americans enjoy today.

The so called Chop Suey houses spread quickly across the country. Originally centered in the Chinatowns of large cities, they began to spread as Americans embraced the new food option. The combination of cheap prices and classy decor proved irresistible to a growing middle class looking to experience the exotic. Eventually, almost every city of any size in the country had a Chinese restaurant and most of the Chinese in the country worked in the industry. The Exclusion Act was not repealed until 1943, but even then the number of Asian immigrants was limited to a quota of 105 per year. This quota was later raised to 2,000 in 1952. The quota system for immigration wasn't abolished until 1965. Today, over 5 million people consider themselves Chinese-American.

#28 Congo Part 1

In 1876, King Leopold II of Belgium dreamed of making his small unimportant country a grand empire to rival the great European powers of the day. However, he was faced with the fact that Belgium was rather poor and that when it came to global empires its people just really didn't give a fuck. To get around this, Leopold formed a fake humanitarian aid organization which funded so called philanthropic expeditions. These expeditions had the actual aim of seizing control of all of central Africa. Eventually catching wind of these shenanigans, the other great powers of Europe freaked right the fuck out. Up until this time, most European powers had been happy enough just trading with the various kingdoms and tribes that controlled the African interior. However, many of the great thinkers of the day had begun warning of a coming Malthusian collapse. Increasingly, people believed that it was only a matter of time before the world ran out of resources, a turn of events expected to result in a just a literal shit ton of famine and war. As a result of Leopold trying to seize control of central Africa, the other European powers realized that the only way to guarantee themselves access to the sweet sweet natural resources of the continent, was to seize control of as much territory as possible before their rivals could. Hence was kicked off what became known as the Scramble for Africa.

It should come as no surprise that the race to claim all of Africa did little to help the European political situation. With the great powers on the brink of war, Leopold came forward to suggest an alternative. Rather than killing each other, the European powers instead in 1885 agreed to carve up the continent into zones of control. This was of course done with absolutely no input from the various kingdoms and tribes already existing in the areas in question. Under the agreement, a large part of central Africa would be left as a neutral buffer zone, which Leopold heroically volunteered to administer. Hence it was that the king of Belgium came to personally own over a million square miles of territory, home to some 20 million people. Leopold named his new personal empire, the Congo Free State.

At the time, none of the other superpowers really wanted the Congo Free State because its territory was rather hard to access and it was widely seen as being devoid of valuable resources. However, this all changed thanks to a rising demand for rubber, which was increasingly being used for various things, foremost amongst them tires for new contraptions like bicycles and automobiles. The Congo Free State was chock full of rubber producing vines, and Leopold found himself sitting on a literal rubber gold mine. All he had to do was find a cost effective way to harvest the rubber. Now if your first thought was to turn the entire region into a veritable slave society, congratulations, you are just as big of a piece of shit as Leopold.

The people of the Congo Free State had long been divided into many different tribes, many of whom didn't really get along with each other. Leopold took advantage of this by selecting a few tribes at random, calling them the Force Publique, and giving them authority to organize the local labor pool. By organize, I of course mean they beat, whipped, and murdered anyone who failed to meet arbitrary quotas set up by pompous business asshats back in Belgium. The whole thing worked rather well as far as Leopold was concerned. He quickly found himself flush with cash, which he mostly spent on fancy monuments to himself and underage prostitutes. However, the various Congolese tribes actually doing the work did not quite agree. The rubber quotas were so large that people in many villages lacked the time needed to actually grow food. When they began to refuse to harvest rubber, the Force Publique upped the ante by torturing people, taking hostages, maiming or killing children, and burning entire villages. Eventually, failure to meet rubber quotas became punishable by death. To ensure that the Force Publique wasn't frivolously wasting bullets on things like hunting, their Belgian bosses began to require the delivery of severed hands to prove they were actually shooting people instead of animals. This resulted in a whole economy forming around severed hands, with many villages attacking each other to collect hands to appease the Force Publique with when they were unable to meet their ridiculous rubber quotas. As with any economy there was innovators, by which I mean some people figured out that they could save bullets by just cutting off living people's hands.

This went on for twenty fucking years. Society pretty much just fell right the fuck apart. The constant violence and inability to farm enough food caused rampant malnutrition, which in turn resulted in a series of epidemics sweeping across the Congo Free State. As the labor pool shrank, by which I mean people dying, the tactics used to ensure quotas were met became more barbaric, which in turn caused further famine and disease in a terrible shit cycle. The nightmare finally came to an end in the early twentieth century after various missionaries and journalists began alerting the world to what was going on. A series of articles, books, and inquiries eventually forced the Belgian government to seize direct control of the Congo Free State in 1908. By that time, half of the region's population had died, some 10 million people. King Leopold and his lackeys were never charged with any crimes. Leopold died the next year of old age.

#29 Congo Part 2

In 1908, the government of Belgium seized control of the Congo Free State from King Leopold II for the little problem of allowing policies that killed 10 million people. Now renamed the Belgian Congo, things instantly got better and everything was super a-okay forever after. Wait, that's not right. In truth, things didn't change all that much. I mean sure, the Belgian government did halt the practice of murdering people for not harvesting enough rubber, but otherwise they continued treating the people living in the region like complete shit. Fun fact, all of the Belgian administrators who had overseen the atrocities were left in place. That's right, not only were they never prosecuted for the terrible things they did, they were also allowed to keep their jobs. I'll let that sink in for a moment.

Now one thing that remained unchanged once things got renamed the Belgian Congo was the idea that the region existed solely for the purpose of supplying money to Belgium. The entire territory was opened to private business interests who diversified the economy away from just rubber to also include the mining of copper and other minerals. The profits from such ventures were all pretty much sent back to Belgium, though some was retained to build railroads, you know, to help export the region's resources faster. To further diversify the economy, wide swaths of land were seized by Belgian investors to create giant plantations to grow agricultural goods for export. Local farmers were also required to grow certain cash crops, you know, in addition to the food they needed to survive. To get labor for all of these enterprises, the Belgian companies paid the locals wages for their work, which though low, provided a better standard of living than what most could expect in their impoverished villages. However, to keep these wages from being too high, the Belgians also brought in a large amount of migrant labor from the surrounding countries.

Being a rather small country, Belgium had to be creative in how it maintained control of its colony. Since just straight up murdering everybody was apparently out, the Belgians instead went with a divide and conquer strategy. The demand for workers scattered tribes from their traditional homelands to more urban areas, diluting tribal power. Belgian authorities also played up and encouraged existing tribal rivalries, ensuring that they would never have to face a unified resistance. The small rebellions that did pop up were quickly put down by the Force Publique. The locals were denied education and a political voice, and were treated like second hand citizens even though they out numbered the Belgians in the territory by a ratio of 130 to 1. This went on for 52 years.

Following World War II, the United States began putting a lot of pressure on its European allies to allow more democracy in their colonies. Though the European powers resisted such ideas, their countries were in ruins, and the Americans had all the money and were threatening to cut off aid to any countries that didn't comply. Giving in, Belgium began programs to expand healthcare and education in the Belgian Congo, and even started letting the locals own private property. This led to a small but growing Congolese middle class who began to agitate for independence. Riots began to break out. Facing the possibility of an all out revolt, which the Belgians lacked the resources to fight, and under increasing international pressure, Belgium granted the Belgian Congo its independence in 1960. It was one of nineteen former African colonies granted independence that year.

Things were ever rosy after that. Okay, actually everything went straight to shit. Though the Belgians agreed to leave, they didn't really do it in a nice way. With the new Congolese government threatening to nationalize the mines in the country, Belgium supported several regions of the country breaking away to form their own countries. The Congolese government turned to the United States for help, but the Americans didn't seem all that interested, so next they turned to the Soviet Union. While the U.S. was down with self-rule in Africa, they most definitely were not down with it if it involved communism. Within a few months, a military coup saw the removal of the so-called communist sympathizers from the Congolese government and the murder of their leader. As a result, the remaining pro-communist officials formed their own government.

The civil war, which was pretty much just a proxy war between the United States and the Soviet Union, lasted for the next five years. By the time what became known as the Congo Crisis came to an end, the country was firmly under the control of a dictator named Joseph Mobutu, a man mostly notable for his love of leopard print hats and his hatred of communism. The newly renamed country of Zaire quickly became a hot bed for corruption, cronyism, economic mismanagement, and human rights abuses. Ironically, one of Mobutu's first moves was to nationalize the country's mines. Despite this, Mobutu received generous support from the United States, which at the time had an official policy of supporting any nut job dictator who was willing to denounce communism. So you know, yea America.

#30 Congo Part 3

With the help of the United States, who were just glad to have someone in power that wasn't a communist, Joseph Mobutu was dictator of Zaire for 32 years, using its natural resource wealth to enrich himself and his cronies. Given that this was a common strategy by the U.S. during the Cold War, it might be good to have a quick aside on the reasoning of the day. By the 1960's, the Soviet Union had been around for about forty years, a time period during which it killed around 16 million of its own people. At the same time, the second most powerful communist nation, China, was well on its way to killing 50 million. In fact, during the seventy years of the communist era the communist regimes collectively killed over 100 million of their own citizens. So yes, while today it's pretty obvious that supporting dictators who killed tens of thousands of their own people was a pretty shitty strategy, at the time it was seen as the lesser of two evils. Whether or not it actually was will likely be debated until the end of time. Anyways, the moment the Cold War ended in 1991, the U.S. mostly got out of the whole supporting dictators thing, leaving Mobutu and his contemporaries on their own. Things of course somehow just got shittier.

The end of Mobutu's dictatorship was tied closely to goings on in the neighboring country of Rwanda. We could spend a whole article talking about it, but here is the cliff notes version. The area today called Rwanda was home to two groups divided mostly economically, the majority Hutu, and the minority Tutsi who held most of the power and wealth. When the Europeans took control of Africa, Rwanda was controlled first by the Germans, but was then given to the Belgians for being on the winning side of World War I. To maintain control over their colony, Belgium worked to keep the Hutu and Tutsi divided, launching a propaganda campaign that they were two separate ethnic groups. This led to the Tutsi generally dumping on the Hutu, which in turn led to a civil war when the Belgians granted the country independence in 1962. The Hutu won the civil war, leading to many Tutsi fleeing to neighboring countries, including a significant number to eastern Zaire. There, they began building up military power with plans to retake the country. In 1990, they began a guerrilla war to do just that. This guerrilla war helped Hutu hardliners gain power, creating a powder keg situation, which erupted in 1994 when the country's president was assassinated, though nobody is sure by whom. Deciding to end the issue once and for all, the Hutus began the systematic killing of Tutsis throughout the country. Within one hundred days, some 500,000 Tutsis were murdered, 75 percent of Rwanda's Tutsi population. In response, the Tutsi rebel army invaded the country, seizing control and killing 300,000 Hutu along the way.

When the Tutsi regained control of Rwanda, around 2 million Hutu, led by the same hard liners who had caused the genocide, took refuge in eastern Zaire. There, they began planning on how to retake Rwanda and started killing Tutsi living in the area. By then Zaire was pretty much a failed state, with especially the eastern half of the country controlled by various resistance groups. In 1996, Rwanda invaded eastern Zaire with the declared goal of protecting the Tutsi in the area. This led to a series of revolts breaking out across the country, which ironically received U.S. support. Eventually, with the help of troops from Rwanda and other neighboring countries, these revolts led to Mobutu being thrown out of power. However, instead of founding a democracy, the rebel leader, a man named Laurent Kabila, declared himself dictator. As all good dictators do, his first act was to change the name of the country, this time calling it the Democratic Republic of the Congo.

Kabila was in a precarious position. It was pretty obvious that his so-called allies from Rwanda and Uganda were planning on seizing control of the valuable mines in the eastern half of the country. To stop them, Kabila ordered all foreign troops to leave, to which Rwanda and Uganda responded by invading again. Things quickly descended into a total cluster fuck from there. Other neighboring countries sent in troops to support Kabila, and numerous rebel and resistance groups sprouted up across the region. The war quickly turned into an all out slaughter, with villages burned, men and women raped, and adults and children forced to join militia units. Both disease and malnutrition ran rampant. In 2001, Laurent Kabila was assassinated, leading to his son, Joseph Kabila, to take power. The following year a peace deal was brokered, officially ending what became known as the Congo War in 2002. Foreign troops left the country soon after, but the resistance groups they had supported remained. Many of these resistance groups continue to fight to this day, committing all sorts of atrocities that have grown worse in recent years. Though the country's first free elections took place in 2006, Joseph Kabila's victory sparked claims of fraud. Kabila was re-elected in 2011, but chose not to run in elections in 2018.

Though little heard of in the United States, the so-called Congo War is the deadliest war to have taken place since World War II. It's estimated that around 6 million people have been killed directly or indirectly by the conflict. For context, it's estimated that the Iraq War cost around 500,000 lives and the Vietnam War resulted in the death of around 2.5 million people. World War II is estimated to have killed some 80 million people. To this day, the Democratic Republic of the Congo is still pretty fucked.

#31 Civet Shit

In the late seventeenth century, traders brought a new type of beverage to Europe called coffee. Prized for its bitter taste and stimulating properties, coffee quickly became a favorite amongst the European aristocracy and rising merchant class. Coffee became a craze that swept the continent, with thousands of coffee houses opening in a relatively short period of time. This of course was accompanied by the usual hand wringing, worrying, and conspiracies from some religious types and folks who in general don't like change. Though rather expensive, many people were more than willing to pay an arm and a leg to get their hands on those bitter aromatic beans. As with anything where there is money to be made, people of course got a little carried away and in general just started acting in as shitty a manner as possible.

At the time of its introduction to the world, coffee was only grown in Ethiopia and Yemen, and its cultivation was a closely guarded secret, you know, because it was worth a butt load of money. However, the high value of coffee eventually attracted the attention of the Dutch East India Company, one of the largest and most powerful corporations in world history. The Dutch East India Company, through a combination of subterfuge and bribes, managed to get their hands on a bunch of coffee plants and took them to the islands of Indonesia, where the company had a stranglehold on international trade and increasingly the islands themselves. Indonesia quickly became the leading source of coffee in the world, a fact that remained true up until the mid-nineteenth century when it was at last eclipsed by supplies from South America. The growing availability of coffee, thanks to increased cultivation throughout the world, eventually made coffee cheap and affordable for the masses, but also helped drive the Dutch East India Company into bankruptcy in 1800. After the bankruptcy, all of the Dutch East India Company holdings, including all of Indonesia, was seized by the Dutch government.

Unfortunately, the Dutch government found itself in much the same situation in Indonesia as the corporation that came before it, namely controlling the islands was costing a shit ton of money. Not being the type to just cut their losses, the Dutch government instead created a system where all Indonesian farmers were required to pay their taxes via exportable luxury crops; namely sugar, indigo, and coffee. This was great for the Dutch since it allowed them to increase exports from the region, but it was not so great for the farmers who suddenly found it difficult to grow enough food for themselves. To add further insult to injury, the Dutch made it illegal for the Indonesians farmers to consume any of the coffee they grew. So you know, all in all it was a pretty fucked up situation.

Now of course the Indonesian farmers were rather curious about the coffee they were growing. After all, anything involving so much bullshit had to be pretty good. This curiosity and the Dutch being shitty people eventually led to one of the strangest workarounds in human history. The Indonesians noticed that a certain cat looking critter called a civet had the habit of eating coffee beans, but not digesting them very well. Yeah, you can probably see where this is going. While the law said Indonesians weren't allowed to pick coffee beans for their own use, it said nothing about picking coffee bean filled shit up off of the ground. They called the coffee brewed from these shit beans kopi luwak, which sounds really creative until you know it's just Indonesian for civet coffee. Now eventually the Dutch colonial officials noticed what the Indonesians were doing, but instead of being grossed out by the whole thing they instead decided to try a cup. Surprisingly enough, the civet coffee was the best tasting coffee they had ever tasted, a fact they attributed to the civet's being rather selective about what beans they ate and possibly something to do with the enzymes in the small animal's gut. Civet coffee quickly became a big hit amongst the Dutch, and fortunes were paid for literally shit.

Now that might have been the end of this story, just a bunch of fancy people drinking shit coffee, but it wasn't. Things actually found a way to become more fucked up. For a time in the early twentieth century, civet coffee was heavily sought after by the rich and powerful of Europe, but the high cost and low supply eventually left it largely forgotten, a curiosity little found outside of Indonesia. That changed at the end of the twentieth century thanks to a combination of the internet, increased world travel, and the rise of Starbucks and other such high end coffee joints. Always on the lookout for the newest crazy thing, people with money in their pockets re-discovered civet coffee and the whole thing went viral. Once mostly forgotten, demand for civet coffee went through the roof as people increasingly felt the need to brag to their friends about how their coffee had come out of some animal's butthole. There was just one little problem, there wasn't enough shit to go around.

With people literally shoving wads of money in their faces, the locals in Indonesia and many other Southeast Asian nations got creative. By which I mean they began locking civets up in tiny cages and force feeding them pretty much nothing but coffee beans. While decidedly bad for the animals, such a practice isn't really all that great for the coffee either considering part of what made it so good was the civet being selective about what beans it ate. Of course none of this really matters given that our brains are wired to assume that if we pay a lot of money for something than it has to be great. Recent campaigns have started to try to end the practice, but have had little effect. Today you can buy kopi luwak for between $100 to $500 per pound.

#32 Unleaded Please

The invention of the internal combustion engine is easily one of the most significant modern innovations of our time. However, early automobiles had a bit of a problem. Without going into too many boring details of how engines work, the basic problem was engine knocking, which is when compressed gasoline auto-ignites rather than getting set off by the spark plug. Engine knocking hurt fuel efficiency and could damage engines. About the only way to counter the problem was to use expensive higher octane fuels, which as one can imagine, did little to increase car sales. This all changed in 1921, when scientists with General Motors discovered that adding lead to gasoline completely removed the knocking problem, allowing for the increased use of cheaper and lower octane fuels. The industry was overjoyed. Car ownership in the United States slowly rose over the next several decades, but really took off after World War II thanks to the fact that the U.S. was the only major industrial power to come out of the war largely unscathed. The resulting economic boom allowed for the fulfillment of the American dream, part of which was everyone and their damn dog owning a car. Things were great, at least until several pesky scientists began pointing out problems.

Starting in the 1950's, scientists began noticing elevated levels of lead in blood tests. Over time these levels continued to rise, quadrupling by the 1970's. This was a bit concerning given that the dangers of lead exposure had been pretty well understood since the early twentieth century. Lead based paint had become widely popular in the U.S. at the time thanks to its cheap price, but growing warnings about its toxicity had led to a sharp decline in its use starting in 1920. For the scientists, the new source of lead seemed pretty obvious, what with every tailpipe in the country belching it out, but it took years of studies to finally convince people that something had to be done. The clincher were studies done in the 1970's showing that children exposed to lead were more likely to develop learning disabilities, have lower IQs, be more aggressive, and have less impulse control for the rest of their lives. Nothing fixes a problem quite like bringing the children into it. Under popular pressure, the U.S. government created new emission standards that over time forced the fuel and automobile companies to find alternative additives to stop engine knocking that weren't so fucking terrible. Unleaded fuels were first introduced in 1979, leading to a rapid decrease in the use of leaded fuels, which were made outright illegal in 1996.

Now that might be very well the end of the story, but it's not. For the rest, we also have to look at other things happening at the same time. Starting in the 1960's, the violent crime rate in the United States began to rise rapidly, doubling by 1970, and then doubling again by 1980. The rapid rise in violent crime caused panic as people began to become convinced that society was coming apart at the seams. Those who were able to, fled urban areas where crime rates were higher. Government officials and the public scrambled for answers; blaming counter cultural elements like hippies, drug use, and the collapse of the traditional American family and values. Vast amounts of money were spent creating and implementing new policies and strategies, but nothing worked. By 1990, violent crime rates were five times higher than they had been in 1960. It seemed as though nothing could be done, but then, for seemingly no reason whatsoever, crime rates began to drop, almost as fast as they had risen.

Of course, a lot of eggheads and policy makers claimed various reasons why the crime rate dropped, but none of the explanations really held up to sustained analysis and the passage of time. It wasn't until recently that the connection started to be made which hopefully you've already figured out. Studies have since shown that lead emission from automobiles can explain 90 percent of the variation in violent crime 20 years later. Generations of kids born into a world with air chocked full of lead particles led to problems that manifested when they became teenagers and young adults. It has been shown that children exposed to lead over their lives are more prone to behavioral problems as a child, pregnancy and aggression as a teen, and criminal behavior as a young adult. Similar correlations between lead exposure and crime have been shown to fit for state data, city data, and even neighborhood data. Though data is less available, some studies have also shown a connection between the rise in use of lead paint in the early twentieth century and the crime wave of the late 1920's and early 1930's. It wasn't just a U.S. problem either. Every country in the world used lead in their gasoline, and though when it was phased out varies, the correlation holds true.

It is frightening to think about how much one thing can affect the world. The overexposure to lead during the mid-twentieth century did not create the world we live in, but it was certainly a factor, the effect of which we will undoubtedly debate and conjecture about for years to come. Pet theories about why crime rates increased abound; including drugs, poverty, the counterculture, and so much racist bullshit. Human behavior is caused by a broad swath of interconnecting inputs all affecting each other in real time, and while it might be fun to try to simplify a problem into a single issue, it just can't be done. The world is far too complex for such things. However, that being said, how much more likely are issues to arise in a world where being dumb, mad, and impulsive is more likely? We may never fully know, but given the plethora of studies that have come out, it seems fair to say that the rise and fall in leaded gas did have an effect on the rise and fall in crime in the developed world in the late twentieth and early twenty-first centuries. If that holds true, it brings up an interesting question of what the future may hold. Though the developed world phased out leaded gas in the 1980's, most of the developing world did not until the 1990's and 2000's. What does the future hold for them, not just in the area of crime, but also in terms of civil wars and terrorism? Only time will tell.

#33 A Little Something About MSG

In 1908, a research scientist in Tokyo named Kikunae Ikeda got his panties in a twist over the taste of the seaweed broth he was eating. Specifically, it drove him nuts that the broth had a flavor that didn't really fit into the existing pantheon of sweet, sour, bitter, or salty. Rather than just moving on his with life, Kikunae instead made up his own flavor, which he called umami, the Japanese word for delicious, and then spent the next year trying to isolate the source of his new flavor. Eventually, Kikunae managed to distill the essence of his umami flavor into a white powder. As you can probably already guess, this powder was monosodium glutamate, also known as MSG by those who don't have the time to not use acronyms.

Within less than a year of being invented, MSG was being manufactured as a food additive. At a time when scientific progress was seen as a good thing, what with humankind giving mother nature and her limitations the finger and all, MSG quickly became a widely used flavor enhancer throughout Japan. It probably didn't hurt anything that MSG was delicious as fuck. Now MSG might have remained a simple curiosity of Japanese cuisine, if it wasn't for the fact that the Japanese were pretty hog wild about invading other countries at the time. Over the next several decades, the Japanese Imperial Army cut a swath through Asia, conquering Taiwan, Korea, and northern China. The people who lived in these places were less than pleased by this turn of events, what with all the wanton crimes against humanity and the such, but they were rather happy with the new delicious flavoring the Japanese brought with them. In fact, the flavoring proved so popular, that it spread beyond the

Japanese controlled territories. Of course, Japanese rule didn't last forever, what with a little thing called World War II, but the popularity of MSG remained. Following World War II, MSG found its way across the Pacific to the United States, first via Chinese restaurants, which had become popular amongst returning American GIs, and then via the big food companies who dumped it in pretty much any processed food they could.

This all changed in 1968, when a recent immigrant from China, Dr. Ho Man Kwok wrote a letter to the New England Journal of Medicine. In his letter, Dr. Kwok, who was from southern China, complained that every time he ate at restaurants serving cuisine from northern China, that he got a headache and felt a numbness in his arms and back and a general feeling of weakness. Dr. Kwok blamed MSG, which at the time was much more common in northern Chinese cuisine. This probably had nothing to do whatsoever with the chemical's Japanese origin or the fact that Dr. Kwok had grown up in China during the Japanese invasion. Now Dr. Kwok had no proof whatsoever, but of course this didn't stop things from getting crazy as shit. Soon after Dr. Kwok's letter, many other doctors also began writing letters to the New England Journal of Medicine describing similar symptoms, which became known as Chinese Restaurant Syndrome. The New York Times eventually noticed all the random talk by prominent doctor types, and ran with the story, of course using a headline written in such a way as to be as racist as possible. Other newspapers ran with it from there, also using super racist sounding headlines, and suddenly everyone and their fucking dog were reporting a growing list of symptoms every time they ate Chinese food, then eventually food from any Asian country.

Of course, all of this was a bunch of bullshit. Even though MSG was heavily used in American processed food, nobody was claiming that they were getting headaches from their can of Campbell's soup. As well, though tens of millions of Japanese and Chinese people had been eating MSG every day for decades, none of them were reporting any problems either. However, this didn't stop Americans from freaking right the fuck out, a situation little helped by the publication of several dubious scientific research papers which linked MSG consumption to a rising list of maladies, including brain lesions and female sterility. Many of these studies were published by a researcher named Dr. John Olney, who became a major advocate of a growing movement of idiots who were calling for the outright banning of the flavoring. In this they were less than successful, probably because of the much more numerous number of studies showing that MSG was perfectly safe. Of course, Olney and his allies in turn claimed that all of these studies were obviously flawed since any researcher who disagreed with them obviously had to be in bed with the big food industry.

Though unsuccessful in getting MSG banned, the whole mess did result in Chinese restaurants across the country changing their recipes to be MSG free in order to avoid the risk of losing business. In comparison, the big food manufacturers continue to use MSG in all sorts of food products to this day, with little to no negative affect on the health of their customers or their bottom lines. Despite close to half of Americans still being convinced MSG is poison as shit, the average American still consumes over half a gram every day.

#34 The Great Stork Derby

In 1926, a wealthy Canadian lawyer and financier named Charles Vance Millar died in his sleep at the age of 73. With no close relatives and a significant fortune up for grabs, his law partners eagerly unsealed the envelope holding his will. What they found was ridiculously horrifying. It's probably a good idea to pause here real quick to mention that Millar was known as a bit of a prankster. One of his favorite hobbies was to leave money on the sidewalk, and then secretly watch as random people scooped it up and furtively pocketed it. The guy was an odd-duck is what we're trying to say. Anyways, Millar's entire will was full of shenanigans. For instance, he gave his vacation home in Jamaica to three men who hated each other, he gave his stock in a brewery to a group of ministers and temperance activists, and he gave his stock in the local horse racing club to a group of anti-horse racing activists. However, it was the last part of his will that gained the most attention. The majority of his fortune, some seven million U.S. dollars in today's money, was to go to whatever woman living in Toronto had the most babies in the next ten years.

Nobody really took Millar's will all that seriously in the early days. Mention of its weird clauses made it into a couple of newspapers, and after that it was largely forgotten. A few of Millar's most distant relatives tried to contest the will, but their efforts really went nowhere. All of this changed in 1932, when the government of the province of Ontario, not liking the idea of seven million dollars just sitting around for a stupid baby making contest, tried to pass a bill that would allow them to seize the money. While the attempt ultimately failed, it did bring the contest back into the public view, and this time a lot of people became very interested, what with it now being the middle of the Great Depression and all.

Now all of this might have been just a strange curiosity if it hadn't been for the Toronto newspapers. Hungry for any story that didn't include standing around in long unemployment lines, the newspapers used public records to hunt down women who had already had six babies over the past six years, dashing to their houses to try and get exclusive interviews. In some cases, the women hadn't even heard of the contest until told by the newspaper reporters knocking on their doors. Dubbed the Great Stork Derby, the press began regularly printing leader boards and interviews with the potential winners, all of which was gobbled up by a public wanting to be distracted by the overall shittiness of their lives. After all, it wasn't an easy time to be living in Toronto, again, because of the Great Depression. Thousands were out of work, a quarter of the population was on welfare, and many families were living in shacks.

The press was unyielding in its coverage of the story, often paying women for the right to write about every little piece of their life. They were of course not kind. Most of the women were poor as shit, and didn't meet the preferred mold of Anglo-Saxon Protestant. Of the front-runners in the race, all were either immigrants, Catholics, and/or women who had children fathered by different men. The newspapers pounced on these poor women, braying about the shitty conditions in which they lived, calling them irresponsible and at times even trollops. The more lurid the descriptions, the more papers that got sold. The women were turned into caricatures. Family tragedies such as stillbirths, miscarriages, and even a baby dying after getting bitten by a rat, were covered in terms only related to how it affected the leader board. The women, desperate for money to help their families, and many planning on having large families anyways, went along with it. Some of the more enterprising used their fame to make money by endorsing products such as soaps. As the years ticked by, the toll on the mothers began to show. Many of the women were constantly in and out of the hospital for operations and transfusions. The infant mortality rate for women involved in the competition was six times the national average. A third of the babies born to these mothers died.

The race finally came to an end in 1936, at which time the front runners all got themselves lawyers to fight for a piece of the pie. A series of court cases ensued in which a judge eventually ruled that in order for a baby to count they couldn't be bastards, they couldn't be stillborn, and they had to be have been properly registered. These stipulations of course mostly affected the poorest of the bunch. Woman after woman was made to testify about every little detail of their personal lives and the deaths of their babies, with the whole traumatic affair punctuated by ribald comments by the rival lawyers. In total, seven women who had nine or more babies were eventually disqualified, leaving just eight mothers, all married middle class Protestants of an Anglo-Saxon background. Parts of the case were appealed and it eventually found its way clear to the Canadian Supreme Court, but in the end the decision was upheld. The four socially acceptable women split the prize, and so ended the Great Stork Derby.

#35 The American Colonization Society

In 1808, the United States outlawed the importation of slaves, ending nearly two hundred years of forcefully shipping people across the Atlantic from Africa. Okay, maybe it didn't completely stop the trade, what with Brazil and several islands in the Caribbean continuing to import slaves for decades, but at least in the United States the practice stopped. Well, at least it stopped being done legally. You know what, we're not going to get anywhere if we get stuck now, so let's just keep going forward with what we got. Anyways, though the international slave trade was made illegal, the trading of slaves already in the United States remained perfectly acceptable, at least up until the Civil War, but hopefully you already know how that whole shindig turned out.

The time following the Revolutionary War in the United States was a time of enlightenment, at least for some. Thanks to the rise of hardcore religious groups, which took a rather negative view of the whole slavery thing, the practice of literally owning people was beginning to look less and less like a good thing. By the time 1808 rolled around, all of the northern states had outlawed slavery, and it had become at least somewhat common for many slave owners to free their slaves upon their death, the slave owner's death that is. As a result, the U.S. was becoming home to an increasingly large number of free black people. This of course caused problems, by which I mean a bunch of asshats created a problem out of nothing. You see, though the abolitionists of the day were totally down with getting rid of slavery, they weren't so down with former slaves living amongst them. Proving that racist ideas just don't change that much, it was claimed that Blacks were mentally inferior savages who had no business mixing and intermingling with the majority white population. Of course, what was anybody supposed to do about it? It wasn't like they could just ship all the freed Black people back to Africa. Oh.....wait......that's exactly what they decided to do.

In 1815, a strange coalition of racist abolitionists, slave owners who really didn't want their slaves noticing that people with the same skin color were walking around free, and free Black people who were just plain sick of getting treated like shit for no good reason, formed the American Colonization Society (ACS). Together, they began working to establish a new country in west Africa, a country that would later become known as Liberia. Though it sounds crazy today, the idea was widely seen at the time as being the best way to handle things. Even good old Honest Abe Lincoln was a major proponent.

Things of course started out all sorts of fucked up. The first thing the ACS needed to do was to buy some land. Luckily, they got a great deal after using the tried and true negotiation tactic of putting a gun to the local chief's head. Colonists began to show up soon after, some 4,500 over the next two decades. These colonists did not have the easiest of times. For one thing, for some reason the local tribes weren't really down with a bunch of total strangers just suddenly appearing and declaring that a big chunk of land belonged to them now. For another, most of the immigrants were several generations removed from their ancestors, meaning that they lacked immunity to the tropical diseases of their ancestral homelands. Between these two factors, around 60 percent or so died. Despite this horrible loss of life, the ACS, which was completely aware of it, just kept shipping more people over, reaching some 15,000 by the start of the Civil War.

In 1847, the Black immigrants formed their own country, naming it Liberia because it kind of sounded like liberty, and forming a government based upon that of the United States. Unfortunately, this involved treating anyone different like shit. The Black immigrants generally viewed the local tribesman as a bunch of filthy savages, and thus refused to grant them citizenship. This didn't change until 1904, though in the mean time they did create a myriad of programs to promote assimilation, by which I mean they forced people to change under the threat of violence. The immigrants also enslaved many of the local tribespeople, a practice that didn't end until the 1930's.

After the U.S. Civil War, the number of African-Americans willing to immigrate to Liberia dropped significantly. As a result, the ACS folded soon after and the idea of avoiding racial assimilation by shipping all the Black people back to Africa died with it. Actually, just kidding, the idea remained politically relevant throughout the early twentieth century, even gaining widespread traction again in the 1920's thanks to Marcus Garvey, a Jamaican born Black nationalist and leader of the Pan-Africanism Movement. The ACS remained an active organization until 1964.

#36 The Farting Fuhrer

Few names bring up a sense of revulsion and disgust quite like the moniker Adolf Hitler. Responsible for the most horrible war in history and a genocide that continues to reverberate to this day, he more than earned his place as one of history's most inhuman monsters. However, it cannot be overstated, no matter what terrible things Hitler did, he was still just a man. Perhaps nothing supports this more than the case of Hitler's farts.

From the time when he was a young man, Hitler suffered from gut issues which periodically wracked him with alternating crippling bouts of constipation, diarrhea, and uncontrollable farting. To make matters worse, the flatulence was reported to be of the type that can only be described as room clearing. As Hitler got older, his gut issues only got worse, a condition that was most likely related to the increasing stresses of his rising political career. Not being the type of person who trusted doctors, Hitler mostly self-treated himself with various over the counter and quack treatments. These attempts at self-care eventually culminated in him becoming a vegetarian, which had the positive side effect of reducing the stinkiness of the farts, but the negative of doubling the volume. He often fled the room after meals to avoid embarrassment. With his guts still wracked by terrible pain, Hitler finally gave in and decided that he needed to see a doctor. As Fuhrer, he had access to the finest medical minds in Germany. However, instead of using these doctors, Hitler went with the recommendation of his personal photographer, who couldn't stop raving about some guy named Dr. Theodor Morell.

It's probably easier to mention right out of the gate that Dr. Morell was most certainly a quack. While the man did have a medical degree, his practice didn't treat real illnesses, instead focusing on handing out supplements to Germany's rich and famous to treat whatever psychosomatic bullshit they felt they had that week. Being better with finances than medicine, Morell was also joint owner of a pharmaceutical company which produced bullshit medicine, the most popular of which was Mutaflor, a pill containing live bacteria cultured from the fecal matter of a simple Bulgarian peasant. Dr. Morell treated Hitler with a handful of vitamins, Mutaflor, and something called Dr. Koester's Anti-Gas Pills. For whatever reason, the Fuhrer decided that this combination of random crap totally made him feel better, and as a result, he made Morell his personal physician.

The elevation of Dr. Morell was not popular amongst the Nazi inner circle, not just because he was a complete quack, but also because he had a habit of constantly belching and farting, not to mention the fact that the man pretty much never bathed. As time went on, Morell began prescribing heavier and heavier doses of his magic pills to Hitler, who for his part, took even more figuring that if a little was great than a lot would probably be awesome. While overdosing on any medication probably isn't the best of ideas, in this case it most definitely wasn't considering the fact that one of the ingredients of the anti-gas pills was strychnine. Though not enough to seriously affect his health, the significant dosage likely did little to help a body already weakened by the stresses of starting a fricking war. As Hitler's ailments began to multiply, so too did the medications prescribed by Dr. Morell, which included injections of bull semen to help boost the Fuhrer's flagging libido. By the time Germany invaded the Soviet Union in 1941, it was estimated that Hitler was taking around 150 pills a week.

It shouldn't really have to be pointed out that if you're stressed out all the time and taking an insane amount of drugs, than you're probably going to feel pretty god damn exhausted. This was certainly true for Hitler, which is probably why Dr. Morell began injecting him with methamphetamine. While originally just for the occasional boost, it quickly developed into Hitler getting at least 2 injections a day, which eventually turned into a 10 injection a day habit. The size of the doses grew too, doubling again and again. Things only got worse as the war dragged on. The high doses of meth began causing insomnia, which left Hitler exhausted, which he in turn treated with more meth. Eventually, Dr. Morell began having trouble finding fresh spots on Hitler's arms to make injections.

Negative side effects began to appear fairly early on. Hitler increasingly began cycling through episodes of euphoria, irritability, paranoia, and impulsiveness; all signs of a toxic meth addiction. At times he would lose complete control of his emotions or become completely obsessed by some small mundane detail. The constant meth use also damaged his cardiovascular system, resulting in several strokes. Eventually, Hitler's inner circle began to question his ability to make rational decisions, but by then it was too late, the Allies were already knocking on the door. By the time Hitler went into his bunker in Berlin, he was reported to have the physical appearance and mental faculties of a very old man. He was only 56 years old. Hitler never emerged from the bunker. As Soviet troops flooded into the German capital, he shot himself.

#37 The Stars Make You Crazy

Tycho Brahe is the father of modern astronomy. His efforts and pedantically annoying insistence on making observations as accurate as possible cleared the way for the works of Galileo Galilei and Johannes Kepler, two men whose work sparked a scientific revolution which continues to this very day. Of course, he was also crazy as shit.

Tycho was born to minor Danish nobles in the mid-sixteenth century. Originally one of a set of twins, Tycho's dear old dad made a deal with his childless brother whereas when the twins were born, one would be handed over to the brother to be raised as his own. Unfortunately, things didn't really go as planned after Tycho's twin brother died soon after being born. Suddenly not having a spare on hand, Tycho's father reneged on the whole deal. This didn't sit well with Tycho's still childless uncle, who after stewing in his anger for two years, simply went over and kidnapped his young nephew. After the deed was done, everyone amazingly enough decided that they were pretty a-okay with this chain of events, which probably had something to do with Tycho's mother recently giving birth to another child. Tycho was raised by his uncle, which was pretty lucky for him given the fact that his uncle was rich as all get out.

Being the heir of a rich ass shit guy, Tycho attended the best of schools, eventually deciding to study astronomy after seeing a solar eclipse at the age of 14. Tycho's uncle wasn't too down with the idea of a career in stargazing, especially since at the time most astronomy was used to make horoscopes. However, Tycho got around this problem by attending university in Germany and lying about what he was studying. This might have caused some problems later, but luckily Tycho's uncle soon after died saving the King of Denmark, Frederick II, from drowning in a river while drunk. Tycho inherited all of his uncle's fortune, which he celebrated by getting into a sword duel with a fellow student over mathematical equations. The duel didn't go so well for Tycho in that his nose got cut off. However, being rich as balls, he simply had a new one made out of brass and attached by glue. Though this being the fifteenth century and all, the glue wasn't that great so his nose kept falling off at inopportune times.

With his studies completed, Tycho returned to Denmark, built himself an observatory, and began making measurements of the movements of the heavenly bodies five times more accurate than the best available observations of the time using tools of his own design. When not sciencing it up, Tycho kept himself busy by knocking up the local minister's daughter, who he was not allowed to marry under Danish law because nobles were not allowed to marry commoners, though it was legally speaking totally cool to fuck and impregnate them. Eventually, Tycho became well known in astronomy circles, which caught the attention of King Frederick II, who wanted Tycho to do his wife's horoscope. Though he wasn't really a believer in astrology, Tycho agreed, probably because doing stuff for the king was never a bad idea. It probably didn't hurt that he started having an affair with the queen soon after. After a few years of these shenanigans, the king gave Tycho an island to build a new observatory and rule as his very own, which is a pretty sweet deal given that most people who aren't kings who fuck queens get their heads cut off.

Tycho built himself a pretty sweet ass observatory and castle on his new island, which included a torture chamber to deal with any of the locals who didn't like his iron fisted and bronze nosed rule. Tycho made his island a major center of astronomy, educating well over a hundred students there over the next several decades. He as well dabbled in alchemy, trying to invent a cure-all medicine, as all learned men of the day did, and threw some pretty crazy parties. To keep himself entertained, Tycho had a half mad dwarf named Jeppe who lived under his dining room table. For god only knows what reason Tycho was convinced Jeppe was psychic and clairvoyant. Tycho also had a tamed 800 pound elk which would follow him around like a dog. Unfortunately, at one particularly wild party, the elk died after getting drunk and falling down a flight of stairs.

Tycho's good times couldn't last forever. When King Frederick II died, his son, Christian IV, proved less than generous. For one thing, he wasn't really a big believer in horoscopes, and for another, he probably wasn't all that happy with Tycho for boning his mother. Not liking the way the winds were blowing, Tycho fled Denmark and took up residence in Prague, where he became court astronomer for the Holy Roman Emperor Rudolf II. Unfortunately for Tycho, in Prague it was customary to not leave the table before the king, which caused some difficulties given that Tycho drank like a fish and the king apparently had a bladder the size of a Buick. After only a few years in Prague, Tycho died of a bladder infection brought on by holding his pee too long. His assistant, Johannes Kepler, soon after stole all of his scientific notes and papers, and as they say, the rest is history.

#38 A Little Something About Self Care

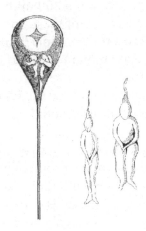

The invention of the microscope in the sixteenth century heralded a new era of scientific discovery in Europe. For the first time, people we would today call scientists began understanding the strange intricacies of the minute details of life. Perhaps one of the most famous of these was a Dutchman by the name of Antonie van Leeuwenhoek. Now Tony ran a draper shop, which is just a fancy way of saying he used to sell cloth for whatever one's cloth needs might be. Back then, pretty much everybody made their own clothes and other such shit, so being a draper could be a pretty lucrative gig. Wanting to get a leg up on his competition, Tony began using microscopes to assess the quality of the fabrics he was buying. Finding the whole idea of microscopes pretty cool, he soon after began looking at pretty much everything he could, designing better microscopes to see smaller and smaller details. Eventually his microscopes got so good that he made a shocking discovery; his glass of water was chock full of tiny fucking animals. Somewhat surprised by this turn of events, Tony began looking at other liquids to see if there was more to see. Yeah, you can probably guess where this is going.

It's probably best not to go into any of the grisly details of Tony's scientific process, so let's just leave it to the imagination. Ahhhh fuck it. The guy masturbated and then took a microscopic peak at what came out. He was more than a little amazed to see millions of tiny tadpoles swimming around, a discovery that sparked decades of scientific debate. Now at the time, many of the so called great thinkers of the day believed in ovism, a weird idea that babies, and all the babies that would ever be, existed fully formed in each of a woman's eggs. This belief stemmed from the discovery that women had eggs, a discovery made several decades earlier by a microscope owning man apparently much more charming than Tony. The whole idea that men weren't the center of the universe made many of the leading scientists of the day, who all just happened to be men, rather uncomfortable. However, the discovery of sperm allowed them to develop a new theory, called spermism, which claimed that sperm were to babies what tadpoles were to frogs. In the end, the theory of spermism won the day, mostly because women's eggs just kind of laid there, while men's sperm wiggled around and went out of its way to prove they were alive.

This turn of events brought up all sorts of uncomfortable questions. For starters, if each sperm was a living baby, didn't that mean it had a soul? And if it did have a soul, was it ethical to go around literally rubbing away some 200 million souls at a time? Second, and even more importantly, where the fuck did all of these sperm come from? Had they existed since the beginning of time? Was there a finite supply? And if so, wasn't going around wasting it just tiptoeing the ever growing human population towards extinction? Now today all of these questions sound pretty stupid, but one has to remember, this was two centuries before people discovered cells and figured out how the whole thing actually works. They were doing the best they could with the information they had.

These questions soon caught the attention of various religious types, who rather than condemn such scientific progress, as was their normal habit, instead fully embraced the new theories, probably because it fit in quite well with their existing belief system concerning having sex for any reason other than making babies. The fact that they could also throw in masturbation to boot, a practice that had previously been seen as a pretty harmless past time, only sweetened the deal for those who loved nothing more than to condemn people willy nilly for silly reasons. The prohibition on male masturbation soon after spread to female masturbation as well, because of course if those religious men couldn't have any fun, why the hell should the ladies?

Eventually, in the early eighteenth century, a quack physician named Dr. Bekker capitalized on the hysteria over masturbation by writing a book claiming that what he called "self-pollution" caused all sorts of terrible ailments, which if taken too far, would eventually lead to death. That's right, there's been asshats writing such books for centuries, and just like today, such books caused all sorts of stupid panics and ideas to run rampant through society. Bekkers made a shit ton of money from his book, and even more from the anti-masturbation powder he also just so happened to sell, sparking a series of copycats who also wrote such books to make money over the next several centuries. Eventually, masturbation became a weird combination of physical disease and mental mania, with even imagining sex becoming taboo since it would only tempt one to give in to masturbatory urges. As time went on, crazier and harsher methods of preventing masturbation were introduced, such as applying leaches to one's genitals. As technology got better in the nineteenth century, leeches gave way to specially made corsets, which in turn gave way to special diets, electroshock treatment, and even castration and female circumcision in severe cases.

Of course, through all of this there were always people who called bullshit on the whole endeavor, but these ideas didn't begin to dominate until the 1950's, when scientific studies began to prove that not only was everybody masturbating, but that it also wasn't killing anyone or even making them sick. Masturbation was declared to be not a mental disorder in 1968, and doctors finally declared it a perfectly normal and healthy thing to do in 1972. However, the topic remains controversial to this day, and even as late as 1994 the U.S. Surgeon General had to resign after suggesting children should be taught about it.

#39 Rastafarians

In 1930, Haile Selassie was crowned the 85th emperor of Ethiopia, a line that claimed direct descent from King Solomon and the Queen of Sheba. It was a pretty big deal, what with at the time Ethiopia being the only original African kingdom not to have been conquered by European powers. The coronation of the new king was welcomed with great celebration in his new kingdom. It was seen as such a big deal that Time magazine plastered it all over the cover of their periodical, including the various ostentatious titles that all emperors are required to have; king of kings, lord of lords, the conquering lion of the tribe of Judah, elect of God, etc. It was these titles that attracted the attention of a poor street preacher in Jamaica, a man named Leonard Howell. Now if you don't know much about street preaching, the key is to get people to actually stop to listen to you, it's kind of the whole point. To get this done, you have to have some kind of a shtick, something like being a very flamboyant speaker, or maybe saying something so crazy that people would stop just to try and figure out how crazy you actually were. Leonard went with the latter, for whatever reason declaring that the new Emperor of Ethiopia was totally the second coming of Jesus Christ.

At the time, Jamaica was home to some 900,000 people of African descent and 100,000 people of British descent. This being the 1930's, you can probably guess who was running the country and what methods they were using. All in all it was a pretty shitty situation. Now for Leonard, though preaching that Haile Selassie was Jesus did totally get the attention of his disenfranchised fellows, it didn't really keep it for very long. After all, if you're poor as shit, Jesus living on the other side of the world is only oh so interesting. To spice things up a bit, Leonard began adding on to his sermons, claiming that not only were people of African descent better than Europeans in the eyes of god, but that god wanted them to return Africa where they would be rewarded with the riches being currently denied them. The promise of a possible better life held people's attention much better, and Leonard began to attract a following. Now at the time, the idea of the descendants of former slaves returning to Africa was not a new one. In fact, a famous Jamaican named Marcus Garvey and his Back to Africa Movement had been espousing such a belief for the past thirty years. Leonard just kind of co-opted it and spiced it up a bit, even going as far as claiming that Garvey was totally a prophet of god or something like that. Garvey, living in London at the time, had no idea that apparently he was now god's voice on Earth.

Eventually, Leonard's street preaching caught the attention of the British authorities, who really not wanting any competition in the royalty department, locked him up for two years for sedition. However, as soon as Leonard was released, he led about a thousand of his followers into the mountains and founded a commune where he and his followers could live the lives they believed they should be living if they were still in Africa. For Leonard, this involved eating only organic and vegetarian foods, having multiple subservient wives, and growing a shit ton of pot to smoke and sell. It was this selling of pot that attracted the attention of the British authorities again, well, that and the stockpiling of weapons for an eventual revolt, and Leonard was thrown into jail again, but was released two years later.

The early years of what became known as the Rastafarian movement were difficult ones, what with Italy invading Ethiopia and overthrowing Halie Selassie in 1936, but when he returned to power in 1941, the movement found new popularity. For many of the poor of Jamaica, it provided a hope that they had never felt before. For their part, the British raided Leonard's commune again and again, eventually completely destroying it and locking Leonard up in a mental institution in 1954. However, it was too late. Rastafarianism had already spread across the Caribbean and into the U.S and U.K. In response to Leonard being locked up, the more militant members of the new religion tried to seize control of Kingston, Jamaica's capital, in 1958. Another violent incident in 1963 led to a major police crackdown. Hundreds of Rastas were arrested, with many tortured or killed while in custody. This caused such a political backlash, that the Jamaican government decided that perhaps it would just be best to try and find ways to get along.

In 1966, the Jamaican government invited Haile Selassie to visit Jamaica. When he arrived, the confused emperor found thousands of Rastas cheering and praising him. Not being one to refuse adoration, he just kind of went with it. Over time the Rastas became less militant as members of the growing middle class joined the movement and subsequent political figures courted their approval. In the 1970's, the reggae music of Bob Marley and his contemporaries spread the ideas of the Rastafarians around the world, though often just the hair and clothing styles, which angered a lot of the religion's actual practitioners. It would be kind of like if rebellious youths started wearing crosses and Catholic priest robes. During this period, the Rastas also attempted to start a community in Ethiopia, but they were met with hostility by the locals who considered them a bunch of foreigners.

In 1974, a terrible famine in Ethiopia resulted in Emperor Haile Selassie being overthrown and imprisoned by a military coup. A year later, he was strangled to death in his bed. This was a bit of a problem for the Rastafarian movement, what with them believing that the second coming of Jesus could not killed. Many members left the movement over the proceeding decades, joining the evangelical Christian sects that were becoming all the rage. Many of the remaining Rastafarians refused to believe that Haile Selassie actually died, even when his body was eventually found buried under his bathroom in 1994. Today there are an estimated million Rastafarians worldwide, and the movement has been credited with creating a sense of collective sense of cultural consciousness amongst the African diaspora. Not bad for a street preacher and a copy of Time magazine.

#40 The Weird Cycle of History

The U.S. presidential election of 1876 was possibly one of the most contentious elections in our nation's history. Widespread cases of fraud in several states led to both parties declaring victory, sparking a constitutional crisis. Eventually, a compromise was hammered out wherein Rutherford B. Hayes, the Republican candidate, was declared the winner. Unfortunately, to get this end, the Republicans had to agree to end the occupation of the former Confederacy, giving them back the full right to govern themselves without the federal government looking over their shoulders. Luckily, the Democrats who controlled these states of course continued the Reconstruction policies that ensured equal rights for all regardless of race. Wait, that's not right. They actually wrote countless laws forcing racial segregation and guaranteeing anyone not White would never get their fair share of the pie.

Now it's probably worth mentioning here that racial segregation was a thing across the United States throughout the era of the 1870's to 1960's. However, for most of the country it was more of an informal system of personal biases and bureaucratic fenangling. The South was more blatant about the whole thing. The moment they were able, Democratic led state legislatures passed a series of bills that became known as the Jim Crow laws. These laws mandated racial segregation at public schools, public places, public transportation, restrooms, restaurants, drinking fountains, and pretty much everything else you can think of. They also made interracial marriage illegal, made it as difficult as possible for non-Whites to vote, and gave individual racists all sorts of opportunities to be just as racist as they could possibly be. It was pretty much a terrible cluster fuck of ways to keep people separate and deny them opportunities, thus making it easier to treat them like shit. So yeah, you know, not exactly the best time in American history.

Anyways, in 1932, far across the Atlantic, a somehow less controversial election led to the nation of Germany getting a new Chancellor. You've probably heard of him. When Adolf Hitler came to power, he set out to fulfill his campaign promises, which unfortunately mostly revolved around turning the country into a dictatorship and doing everything in his power to segregate and destroy Germany's Jewish population. Now at the time, Jewish people were not only pretty well integrated into German society, they were also doing pretty well for themselves, two things that just set Hitler's anti-Semitic blood to boiling. Not really knowing the best way to go about undoing these things, he and his fellow piece of shit Nazis began looking around for a similar system upon which to base their own. You can probably guess the one which most caught their attention. That's right, the U.S.'s fucking Jim Crow laws. We all know what happened next. The Jewish people of Germany, and then conquered Europe, found themselves facing harsher and more restricting laws, eventually leading to the ghettos, and then the horrors of the Holocaust. This all started in the 1930's, with a series of laws that disenfranchised Jewish people and barred them from certain jobs, civil and academic positions being top of the list. Not really being down with this whole turn of events, and sensing the coming trouble, many Jews chose to flee Germany, many to the United States.

Now at the time, the U.S. didn't really have a refugee policy, just a super restrictive and racist immigration policy which only allowed in so many of each "type" of person each year. As a result, only so many Jewish people fleeing from Germany were able to get into the U.S., with priority given to those who were seen to have valuable skills, such as university professors. Now some of the more famous of these professors, such as Albert Einstein, found the U.S. to be a very welcoming place. Unfortunately, this was not true for the not so famous professors, who upon arriving, found that anti-Semitism was totally a thing in the United States as well. Despite many having some pretty fantastic credentials, the major American universities wanted nothing to do with them. As a result, most of these Jewish academics ended up getting whatever teaching jobs they could get, with many ending up in the South teaching at various colleges set up by the disenfranchised Black community.

Thus it was that the strange flows of history created a situation where the severely underfunded Black colleges of the American South were given access to professors who would have seen such positions to be beneath them if conditions had been different. Thousands of students were taught by these professors over the proceeding decades, gaining access to a level of education that they might not have otherwise had. This led to better trained African-American academics and more members of the Black community clawing their way up into the American middle class, which in turn helped foster the growth of the Civil Rights movement, which eventually resulted in the desegregation of schools in 1954, the Civil Rights Act of 1964, and the Voting Rights Act of 1965; ending the Jim Crow era.

Professor Errare Presents....45 Jerks and Counting

A jocular rant going over the quirks and foibles of the forty-five jerks that somehow convinced us it would be a good idea to let them lead our nation.

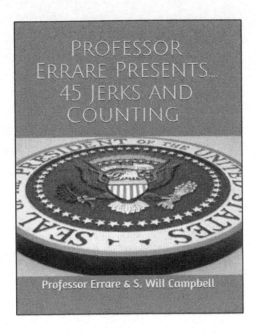

Professor Errare Presents....40 American Jackasses Worth Knowing

American history is full of jackasses, unfortunately many of them have been forgotten. Professor Errare proudly presents forty of them that are well worth remembering.

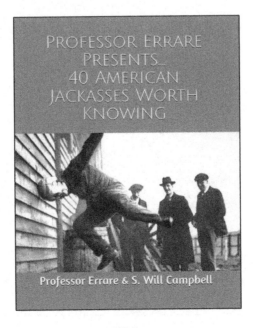

Professor Errare Presents….And Then What Happened

Hey have you heard about that famous event….well guess what, that's not the most interesting thing about it. Don't believe us? Check out this shit.

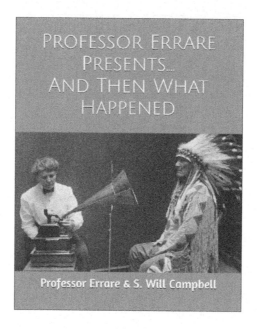

Professor Errare Presents….Random History

Who needs patterns? I'll tell you who doesn't, people who like random history thrown at them with absolutely no rhyme or reason connecting any of it.

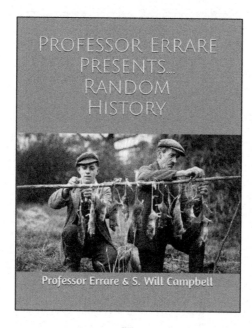

Want more Professor Errare? Are you still thirsty for knowledge? Professor Errare runs a weekly updated blog of the same name with all sorts of tidbits for your perusing. You can find it here:

http://www.facebook.com/professorerrare/

or

http://www.shawnwcampbell.com/errare/

About The Authors

Professor Errare is a world renowned cynic with a degree in bullshit from the University of None Of Your Damn Business. Professor Errare is a proponent of old school history, where the historian does not let things like facts or other opinions get in the way of a good story. Professor Errare hopes that this book generates some income because you can't get coke and hookers for free. He currently runs a blog by the same name where he provides a weekly dose of knowledge.

S. Will Campbell has absolutely no interest in history, but he does know how to type, which is a necessity given that Professor Errare lacks this skill. S. Will Campbell wants nothing to do with Professor Errare, but a collection of sleazy photos that could easily get put on the internet keeps him in line. S. Will Campbell's crippling anxiety keeps him from having a wife and kids, or even pets, but he does have a nice house plant named Morton that keeps him company.

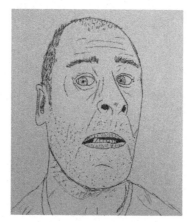

Made in the USA
Columbia, SC
17 September 2020